The Narratives of Michel Butor

THE WRITER AS JANUS

THE NARRATIVES OF

MICHEL BUTOR

The Writer as Janus

by
Dean McWilliams

Ohio University Press

95,058

For my parents
and Alvi

Contents

Preface

The Writer as Janus

*Literature is a transcription
suspended between a past
which must be preserved
and a future
which must be prepared.*[1]

Janus, the Roman god of beginnings, presides over Michel Butor's
many writings. This legendary two-headed figure, met by Léon Delmont
in the dreams which climax *La Modification*, Butor's most famous
novel, simultaneously looks back over the past and ahead to the future.
For Butor, yesterday and tomorrow are dialectically related: it is only by
uncovering the forces buried in the past that the present can be understood and the future prepared. His protagonists dig back through their
earlier lives, searching the roots of their current dilemmas. But these
roots must always be traced further, deep into the cultural subsoil from
which our civilization has sprung. The struggle to understand contemporary society by excavating our collective past is the guiding theme
of Butor's work. His ten major narratives form a schematic and chronological exploration of Western civilization and its component cultures
from ancient Egypt to contemporary America. More recent texts consider the future: these Utopian speculations are closely related to the
dominant historical theme since Butor's discoveries in the past help
define his desiderata for tomorrow.

I have chosen Butor's excavation of our past as my primary focus
for several reasons. First, it lies at the heart of his work. To be sure, no
single perspective allows us to see all of an author's writings with equal
clarity; all the more so in the case of this artist whose work includes
novels, poetry, theory, criticism, opera, and multi-media performances.
And yet, Butor's novels and longer narrative texts are surely the most
important and substantial part of his work; and this historical exploration is the primary uniting theme of Butor's major narratives. To borrow
another of Butor's mythic metaphors, it is my belief that this topic can
serve as an Ariadne's thread supple enough to lead the beginning
student through all of Butor's major works and strong enough to draw
together the experienced scholar's many impressions. Although I will

treat each of Butor's longer narratives in more or less chronological order, my primary loyalty is to the developing historical exploration; thus I will depart from strict chronology to introduce material from other texts if they illuminate a particular stage in Butor's examination.

This historical theme has a further advantage. The vision of man as a product of history has been the modern novelist's greatest inheritance from the realist masters and, in the light of recent history, his greatest burden. My discussion of Butor's own attempts to understand modern man's relationship to his past will take him out of the limiting confines of the French avant-garde and place him in the broader and more illuminating context of the continuing international development of modernist and postmodernist fiction.

I would like to publicly thank the following individuals and institutions: Ohio University Research Committee and the Camargo Foundation for financial support; the editors of *University of South Carolina French Literature Series* and *L'Esprit Créateur* for permission to reprint in my introduction and chapters three and eight material that originally appeared in these journals; the staffs of Alden Library, Ohio University and of the Bibliothèque Municipale de Nice for bibliographical assistance; Leon Roudiez for reading and commenting helpfully on a paper that has been incorporated in the introduction and chapter eight; Roland Ball, Chandler Beall, Thomas Hart, Elinor Miller and Rainer Schulte for their learning and friendship. Finally I wish to express my gratitude to Michel Butor for interviews conducted in 1970, 1974 and 1977.

Introduction

Butor's Past

Michel Butor was born 14 September, 1926 in Mons-en-Barouel near Lille, France, the fourth of seven children in a devoutly Catholic family. The Butors moved to Paris when Michel was three, settling first in the rue du Cherche-Midi and then, in 1936, in the apartment at 107 rue de Sèvres, where Butor twenty years later received reporters after winning the prestigious Prix Renaudot. Butor, keenly sensitive to the power of a place, would surely approve if we looked more closely at the world in which he spent his formative years. He grew up in that area of Paris where the sixth and seventh arrondissements meet on the eastern fringe of the Latin Quarter. The rue de Sèvres is a busy commercial street, crowded with a major department store, shops, and apartments and near the parochial school Butor attended: in many ways a typical middle-class Parisian neighborhood. But it is also close to the university, literary cafés, and student haunts that for centuries have made Paris Europe's intellectual capital. A curiously divided world: if Butor's heroes often seem pulled between bourgeois comfort and free-thinking bohemianism, they reflect his own ambivalent beginnings.

Butor's lycée years were also the years of the German occupation. The country's depressed intellectual life and his own boredom with school routine turned Butor inward. He read deeply in the family library of alchemical arcania, studied Kafka, Joyce, Proust, and Faulkner, and associated with an important group of philosophers and intellectuals who gathered at the Château de la Fortelle. During these school years, Butor began writing poetry, deeply influenced by André Breton and the surrealists.

In 1944 France was liberated and Butor entered the University of Paris. He had spent an extra year in the lycée in order to prepare for entrance into the Ecole Normale Supérieure but abandoned this plan to study instead for a *licence* in literature at the Sorbonne. He found, however, that his wide-ranging intellectual appetites were poorly suited for this program and switched to philosophy, earning both a *licence* and a *diplôme d'études supérieures*. These were, of course, the years when existentialism was on the rise in France. Jean-Paul Sartre, more than anyone else, spoke for the postwar French intellectuals. Butor responded to Sartre's call for intellectual rigor and personal engagement: "Sartre was a philosopher and we needed a serious literature; the only literature which could matter for us was a literature helping us to make a map or a relief of reality, a literature helping us to see and to understand what remained among the ruins, what was solid."[1]

Although a serious and committed student, Butor seems to have been unable to confine his intellectual curiosity to academic reading lists, and he twice failed in the national competitive exams for the *agrégation en philosophie*. Then, in 1950, he accepted a position teaching French in El Minya, Egypt, a decision which proved crucially important in his literary career. The Nile Valley's time-scarred monuments deeply impressed him, drawing him back seemingly to the time of the Pharaohs and stimulating further his interests in travel and in the past. These two interests are really one, since for Butor, "to travel from one place to another is also to travel from one historical depth to another."[2] Each of the many places Butor has visited has had a characteristic "génie du lieu," a unique ambience created by the history of the place. Butor has sought through careful attention and study to describe these historical forces. His geographical and temporal wanderlust has led him all over the globe and into every era of European and American history. He began his first novel, *Passage de Milan* (1954), while living in the Nile Valley. In it he tried to capture the strange retrospective light which his Egyptian experience cast on his earlier Paris years.

Butor discovered that teaching abroad enabled him to combine travel and literature in a profession that offered time for his own writing. Thus he became, in his own words, "a traveling salesman of French culture." He spent 1951–53 at the University of Manchester, England, using his vacations to explore Tunisia, Algeria, and Italy. After a year translating in Paris, he left again in the fall of 1954, this time for Salonika, Greece, where he taught and traveled to Crete, Delphi, and Istanbul. While in Greece, he began work on his second novel, *L'Emploi du temps* (*Passing Time*). Although his first novel passed virtually unnoticed, his second effort was more successful, winning the Prix Fénéon in 1956. True literary notoriety arrived when his third novel, *La Modification* (*A*

Change of Heart), won the prestigious Prix Théophraste Renaudot in 1957. Butor's fourth novel, *Degrés* (*Degrees*, 1960), was more controversial, but his first volume of critical essays, *Répertoire* (*Inventory*), published the same year, won the Prix de la Critique Littéraire. These successes brought new publishing arrangements, greater security, and more international speaking and teaching invitations.

In 1960 Butor, now married, came to the United States to teach at Middlebury and Bryn Mawr Colleges. He was fascinated by what he saw: coming up for the first time out of a subway into an American city, Butor literally staggered under the impact of the colors, lights, and sounds. The fascination has continued, drawing Butor back to teach at the Universities of Buffalo and New Mexico and producing a series of American texts including *Mobile* (1962), *6.810.000 litres d'eau par seconde* (*Niagara*, 1965), and *Où, Le Génie du lieu, 2* (*Where/Or, The Spirit of the Place, 2*, 1971). Butor has also taught in the French universities at Vincennes and Nice. In 1973 he gained the academic confirmation that earlier had been denied, receiving the *doctorat* and defending as his thesis his critical work. During the sixties and seventies Butor's growing international reputation and his interest in the arts drew him into collaborations with numerous artists. With painters and printmakers he produced a series of *Illustrations* which mingle poetry and art, and with composer Henri Pousseur he helped to create an opera *Votre Faust* (*Your Faust*).

No account of Butor's past could be complete without mention of his literary "ancestors." "Every writer," Jorge Luis Borges tells us, "creates his own precursors." Of few writers is this more true than of Butor, who has deliberately and assiduously studied a series of literary masters with the conscious intention of learning from them. The title of his four critical collections indicate Butor's relationship to the subjects of these essays: *Répertoire* means a catalogue or list, but it is also the root of our "repertory" and denotes a body of material that has been thoroughly mastered and can be performed at will. The impressive range of Butor's literary interests is indicated by the more than forty authors, from many languages and every period, treated in these articles and in three additional book-length studies. Among these, several appear to have been especially important in Butor's literary formation. Rabelais, Montaigne, Hugo, Balzac, Baudelaire, Proust, Joyce, and Faulkner have each been the subject of at least two essays or a book-length study. To these we must add several other authors whom Butor has personally acknowledged as important influences: Melville, Flaubert, Mallarmé, and Henry James.

Butor's Purposes

There is a deep and rigorous humanistic commitment in this teacher-scholar-writer who chose the Renaissance, nineteenth-, and twentieth-century masters as his tutors. Butor shares with his "ancestors" a dedication to literature as a means of achieving human understanding and freedom: "The role of the novelist," Butor tells us, "is to lead to a clarification, to permit an awareness of the problems which preoccupy us." Serious writing seeks "the transformation of the mental tissue within which we live, within which we are submerged, of the system within which our freedom finds its references for action."[3] " 'We must change life,' " Butor insists; "any literature which does not aid us in this purpose . . . is ineluctably condemned."[4]

Butor's commitment to literature as a means of transforming our consciousness directs both the form and the content of his narratives. Much of what we know of the world comes to us through language: books, newspapers, conversations, etc. The verbal information we receive is inevitably shaped and influenced by the forms that we use to organize it. When we use inadequate narrative structures we risk obscuring the significance of our experience: key events are missed, insignificant ones dramatized. We feel this inadequacy when we are unable to arrange our experience into meaningful patterns. Jacques Revel (*L'Emploi du temps*) and Léon Delmont (*La Modification*) both struggle toward a self-knowledge that comes only after they find new and more revealing structures with which to organize their memories of the past. Butor feels that the serious writer has an obligation to help develop structures by means of which we can better recount our own lives.

Butor's strenuously experimental structures serve very serious purposes, a fact which must be understood if they are to be seen as more than gratuitous literary exercises. He vigorously opposes "art for art's sake" aestheticism which ignores the content of an artist's vision not only in literature but in painting and music as well.[5] He views his narrative experiments as "didactic or pedagogical structures"[6] which teach us to see the world differently. His disruptions of linear narrative chronology, beginning with his second novel, force us to recognize the relationship between seemingly isolated moments in the past and present. His textual collages, which begin in his fourth novel and become increasingly important thereafter, break up familiar, quasi-canonical texts to highlight important details and to juxtapose them, often ironically, with other texts and occurrences. Butor's formal experiments attempt to show us something about the world, and thus content is tremendously important. Form and content are, of course, never completely separable: form enables us to see and, in the process, becomes part of the vision. Still, the manner of seeing exists not for its own sake but for what it shows us of the world: to resist the thematic content of Butor's narratives is to resist the movement to consciousness that they are meant to effect. "The book," Butor tells us, "is for me a way to know the world and to act on it. . . . To limit oneself, as some have done, to one's discipline, to one's art, is to refuse reflection, is to choose stupidity and to reduce this art to nothing more than a craft. For me, to create literature is to occupy oneself *openly* with the world."[7]

Pressed by an interviewer to identify his principal theme, Butor offered "universal history."[8] Butor's narratives confirm this suggestion: the subject to which they continually return is man's relationship to the past. One of Butor's favorite metaphors for the literary artist is the "mental archeologist"[9]: his travel essays and narratives are "excavations" of the historical forces buried within a particular site. Understanding of the past is crucial to Butor's goals of consciousness and freedom. Without this knowledge man is a prey to forces he only dimly comprehends: an individual "who is ignorant of everything that has led to the situation in which he finds himself, cannot achieve self-understanding. He is, in a sense, exterior to himself and his conduct will seem an inexorable fate."[10] Characters who evade this awareness inevitably suffer the consequences. In *Passage de Milan*, Jean Ralon struggles to close the door on the ancient Egyptian ghosts who threaten his Christian faith; *Mobile*'s white Americans try to efface their continent's Indian past. These attempts to escape the past fail: the dispossessed deities return to haunt the fitful sleep of Butor's characters.

Ancient civilizations retain their power in our psychic lives because they represent authentic human possibilities—ways of living different from present modes which have nonetheless been realized in the lives of earlier generations. To turn our backs on those past achievements is to turn our backs on parts of ourselves, to repress important possibilities within our personalities. The excavation of ancient cultures buried within our past is thus not only an *historical* activity, but more important, a *psychological* activity—the exploration of our own human potential. "It is for this reason that we are archeologists: to know who we are and what we have forgotten, lost while still retaining it; to find or discover our own, unknown face."[11]

The full understanding of our true selves is essential to the deliberate preparation of the future; thus we are led to the paradox at the center of Butor's historical interests: "What we seek in archeology is not so much our past as our future, because what causes the birth of such a vocation is the fact that ancient works appeared to us as precious models, rich in contemporary instruction; and naturally it is not merely a matter of isolated works most of the time, but of ways of living which, in relation to our present way of living, open new possibilities. The wonder that we feel among Rome's ruins or those of Crete comes from what they inspire for changes in our homes, towns and mores."[12]

Seen in light of his historical excavation of our collective past, Butor's narratives have a remarkable schematic coherence. They begin chronologically with the earliest components of our culture and move gradually forward. *Passage de Milan* explores the role of ancient Egypt in the lives of modern Parisians, and *L'Emploi du temps* analyzes the relationship of a series of ancient, classical, and Christian cultures buried within modern industrial society. *La Modification* investigates Imperial and Christian Rome, while *Degrés* focuses on Europe during the Renaissance and Age of Discovery. *Description de San Marco* and *Portrait d'artist en jeune singe* add supplementary details to the European fresco, discussing Byzantine and medieval Europe. The American texts (*Mobile, 6.810.000 litres d'eau par seconde*, and *Où, Le Génie du lieu, 2*) examine America's place in "universal history." *Intervalle*, Butor's most recent narrative, scrutinizes contemporary European culture.

Butor's Mythic Structures

Butor's essays and interviews state his intentions clearly. But purposes must be checked against literary practices: what matters in the final analysis is not what Butor states but what he does. The basic situations and structural patterns which recur throughout Butor's narratives are in this respect extremely useful, corroborating and illuminating the intentions explained in his essays.

Butor's novels and texts abound in references to Egyptian, Greek, Roman, and American Indian myths; more revealing for our present purposes is his use of the "monomyth," the narrative pattern that Joseph Campbell finds in all the world's great myths: "the standard path of the mythological adventure of the hero is a magnification of the formula represented in the rites of passage: *separation—initiation—return.*"[13] The protagonist ventures forth from the world of common experience into a new realm where he is tested and wins a victory for himself and his community. The initiation motif is, of course, universal in its appeal, and its presence in Butor's novels would not of itself be particularly surprising. What is significant is, first, the way Butor manipulates certain of its structural elements and, second, the very persistence of these patterns: they appear not only in the novels but also in experimental narratives and critical-creative texts.

The mythic initiate acts, Joseph Campbell reminds us, not only for himself but also for the social group of which he is a part: "the hero comes back from the mysterious adventure with the power to bestow boons on his fellow man."[14] It is important to emphasize the social benefits derived from the individual initiation, for the rites of passage blend easily with the seasonal festivals of communal regeneration to which they are morphologically related. The initiatory pattern, like the vegetation ritual, imitates the rhythm of withdrawal, disappearance, and reappearance seen in the natural movements of the sun, moon, and seasons. Initiation and fertility rites perform on different levels the same integrative and regenerative functions: "rites of initiation and installation . . . teach the essential oneness of the individual and the group; seasonal festivals open a larger horizon. As the individual is an organ of society, so is the tribe or city—so is humanity entire—only a phase of the mighty organism of the cosmos."[15] The boy is reborn as a man and the man as a priest through the initiatory ordeals; society itself is regenerated and time renewed by the rebirth of the seasons. Butor exploits both the integrative and regenerative potential of this mythic pattern of separation, initiation, and return.

Butor's narratives characteristically begin with the isolation of his protagonist in one of two ways. The main character is most often cut off from his native milieu and set adrift in a foreign culture (*L'Emploi du temps*, *La Modification*, *Portrait d'artiste en jeune singe*, *Mobile*, *6.810.000 litres d'eau par seconde*). In other instances, he is cut off within his own society by social stigma (*Passage de Milan*) or by the pressures of his work as a writer (*Degrés*). Separation prepares Butor's protagonists for the "initiatory ordeal *par excellence*"[16]: the descent into the underworld. This trial, seen most clearly in the references to Theseus, Orpheus, Aeneas, and the Egyptian *Book of the Dead* in the novels, is endured, either literally or metaphorically, by all of Butor's heroes. The descent occurs on several levels. There is usually a physical penetration of a subterranean passage or a darkened interior. Louis Lécuyer wanders in the cellar beneath 15 Passage de Milan, and Léon Delmont's train enters Mont Cenis tunnel at a crucial stage in his journey. Butor blunders into a strange underground world in the dreams recounted in *Portrait*, and the "pilgrims" at Niagara twice journey into the gorge beneath the falls. Two protagonists repeat Theseus' tracing of the labyrinth: Jacques Revel penetrates the darkened maze of Bleston's streets, and Butor follows the winding through the interior of San Marco. The principals of *Intervalle* interrupt their night journey, descend from their trains, and enter the cavernous interior of the Lyon-Perrache train station. Pierre Vernier's descent into sickness and, we assume, the grave, in *Degrés*, is the most literal and final of these voyages to the underworld.

Two interiors on this physical itinerary are particularly significant in Butor's historical quest—the museum and the place of worship. Museums like those studied in Bleston (*L'Emploi du temps*), Rome (*La Modification*), and Bavaria (*Portrait d'artiste en jeune singe*) reveal both what a culture wishes to preserve and what, by exclusion, it wishes to obscure in its past. Churches and cultic places are perhaps even more useful. Bleston's Old Cathedral, the Vatican's Sistine Chapel, and Venice's San Marco present in their decorations synoptic visions of their culture's past and future.

This physical exploration occurs simultaneously with several other voyages into darkness. Butor's seekers journey into themselves, first, by consciously dredging up past memories and, then, by confronting the repressed desires revealed in their dreams. The descent into the unconscious is not just into an individual's personal memories and complexes but into those of an entire culture. Butor warns those who would psychoanalyze the dreams experienced by the characters in his novels and texts that: "all of this has significance only within the context of a historical analysis, in relation to universal history."[17] The personal descent leads to the important historical descent into our cultural past.

The models which all Butor's protagonists seek to emulate are Aeneas, Léon Delmont's hero in *La Modification*, and Adoniram, the Nervalian figure who appears in Butor's Beethoven *Dialogue*. These mythic champions descend to the center of the earth to meet their ancestors and learn from them the secrets of the past and the future. Butor's characters seek that visionary moment when chronology is broken and time becomes spatial: significant but forgotten moments are juxtaposed, and their relationship to each other and the present is understood. The effect of such a moment would be both intellectual and volitional, freeing us to act. The goal sought by Butor and his protagonists is that "all history would become luminous and, as a consequence, we would know what we want."[18]

Their ordeal complete, Butor's voyagers return, transformed, to the outside world. Delmont goes back to Paris a nascent novelist, and Louis Lécuyer and the Butor of the *Portrait* will begin new lives in Egypt. Pierre Vernier dies before having completed his journey, but we will discuss his apparent failure later.

It is in the context of this ritual pattern of withdrawal, initiation, and return that the unique temporal rhythm of Butor's narratives is best understood. We have already spoken of the way in which this primitive pattern mimics the natural rhythms of the sun and the seasons. We recognize these same rhythms in the temporal unities of the day and the year around which Butor organizes his narratives, as the following schema indicates:

	Day	Year
Passage de Milan	7:00 P.M.–7:00 A.M. key events around 4:00 A.M.	
L'Emploi du temps	Revel writes journal at night	1 Oct. to 30 Sept.
La Modification	8:10 A.M.–5:45 A.M.	15–16 Nov.; four of past voyages also in fall
Degrés		Oct. 1954 to Nov. 1955 but primary emphasis on Oct. to Jan.
Réseau aérien	Approximately 36 hours, alternating sections of night and day, ends at night	
Mobile	3:00 A.M. EST to 12:00 P.M. MST (2 A.M. EST), 48 hours	Occurs at the vernal equinox
Description de San Marco	Begins at midday ends at sunset	
6.810.000 litres d'eau par seconde	8:00 A.M. to 2:00 P.M. 2 1/2 days	April to March
Portrait d'artiste en jeune singe	Central section alternates 8 days and 7 nights, Mon. to Mon.	Covers seven weeks
La Rose des vents, 32 Rhumbs pour Charles Fourier	Organized around 24-hour cycle of rising and dying light. Begins and ends in night	Each stage represents a different point in the year. Begins and ends in winter
Dialogue avec 33 variations de Ludwig Van Beethoven Sur une valse de Diabelli		Each variation represents different point in year. Begins and ends in winter

Où, Le Génie	Begins in morning;	Nov. 1966 to
du lieu, 2	ends at night	Dec. 1969
Intervalle	8:30 P.M.–12:05 A.M.	Butor's journal begins in July and ends in Nov.

The schema also indicates the manner in which Butor shapes these unities to emphasize the hours of darkness. Each narrative contains a substantial, sometimes even a predominant, portion of the dark hours or months of the day or year. It is usually during these times of darkness that the crucial descent into the self occurs. The chronological movement of time within the narrative thus accentuates the descent motif seen in the actions of the central characters.

It is significant, in addition, that Butor terminates his narratives in times of darkness. The narratives that occur over one or several days most often end in the early morning hours. Those works based on the unity of the year usually conclude in the waning light of autumn or in winter. Butor ends the voyage in darkness and compels his readers to continue on their own. He wishes to force his readers into an involvement in his fictional situations and, through them, into a consideration of their own real situations. Thus it is very much to his purpose that his works be open and, to a certain degree, incomplete. He deliberately leaves his readers in darkness, both literal and metaphorical, in order that they be required to continue the process begun by his fiction. The classic quest described by Campbell is circular, but Butor offers us "not the closed circle to which we can add nothing, but the spiral which invites our pursuit."[19]

The descent into the past can never be a nostalgic return to a comfortable tradition which then becomes the center of our lives. On the contrary, it is often an unmasking of our fraudulent ideas about the past, forcing a reevaluation of our present situation. The voyage underground, Butor explains, "returns us to the surface on the other side of the normal horizon, denounces that surface as a lie. It is a matter of a reversed, reversing ascent, where the point of arrival situates the point of departure by making it undergo a reorientation (this is why this point of arrival is so often conceived of as a center), by forcing it to make a confession."[20] The return to the past is not merely destructive; it can suggest fruitful possibilities which may be adapted and assimilated but never naively embraced as an all-answering panacea. Butor unites us briefly with our sources only to break the umbilical cord once again and force us to use our freedom in the preparation of a better future.

There is always an ironic gap between Butor's protagonists and their mythic models: Jacques Revel is not Theseus, nor is Léon Delmont Aeneas. For them to be so and for their quest to succeed fully would require that our civilization indeed have a center, a notion effectively contradicted by all of Butor's narratives. Thus Revel's and Delmont's victories are partial and perhaps only temporary; Vernier's failure is total.

But what is seen as a defeat in the individual lives of these fictional characters appears different when viewed on the collective level of the reading audience. Seen in the context of the ritual renewal of the community, Butor's frustrated heroes are scapegoat victims. Butor's remarks about Vernier can be applied to all his protagonists: "There had to be this sacrifice within the novel. Insofar as he accepts . . . being this victim, he succeeds. Insofar as he realizes that 'that future music' is denied him but that his death will render it possible for others, he is entirely forgiven."[21] Butor's protagonists are like another mythic figure encountered by Léon Delmont: Moses, "who points out the Promised Land, but who will not enter it himself; it is because he cannot enter it that he is capable of showing it to others. . . . They reach it not with their body, but with their spirit, and they are in communication with the future."[22] But even here the ironic gap is still great. The future is distant and opaque; there are no assurances that Vernier's writings will, like Marco Polo's journals which he so much admires, provide the impetus for future discoveries.

There is a fundamental tension within Butor's work. His characters inevitably meet with disappointment, and their journeys end in darkness. Despite this fact, Butor returns again and again to the oldest and most basic of ritual patterns: the rites of personal and collective regeneration. The very persistence of this structure underscores Butor's faith, often challenged but never defeated, in the power and importance of literature: "I believed, yes, I believed that the world's fate depended, in a very small way of course, but depended nonetheless on what I wrote, and when I am imprisoned in the depths of my writing, I believe it still."[23]

CHAPTER 1

Passage de Milan

Butor's first collection of travel essays carries as its frontispiece a picture of the Fontaine du Fellah, located in the rue de Sèvres in Paris. This imitation of an ancient Egyptian statue, standing incongruously in the heart of the neighborhood where Butor was raised, could also serve as the frontispiece or cover of his first novel, *Passage de Milan* (1954). The novel's title refers both to the Parisian street in which the principal characters reside and to the passing of the kite, or *milan*, symbol of the Egyptian god Horus. The title thus directs our attention to the novel's main theme, the meeting of modern Paris and ancient Egypt. The Fontaine du Fellah is even more appropriate in that this rigid male figure stands at the head of the steps leading down into the Parisian subway: several of the inhabitants of the apartments at 15 Passage de Milan will descend, in the course of the novel, deep into the Egyptian underworld.

Butor begins his historical excavations in a seemingly ordinary Parisian apartment building on an evening during which a birthday party is being given for one of the residents. Before the novel's twelve hours have run their course, powerful forces will erupt from beneath this placid surface, leaving the party's guest of honor dead and drawing other residents into contact with the historically and geographically remote world of Egypt. The apartments at 15 Passage de Milan offer a microcosm of contemporary Parisian society. The concierge and his wife on the first floor and various servants throughout the building represent the working class. The second floor's Mogne family and the fourth floor's Vertigues family are members, respectively, of the lower and upper middle classes. Other residents include a Jewish intellectual (Samuel Léonard on the third floor), a young artist and his wife (the De Veres on the fifth floor), and two Catholic priests (Jean and Alexis Ralon on the first floor). A member of the nobility, a German prince, makes a token appearance at Angèle Vertigues's birthday party, rounding out this social portrait.

Butor's scarcely veiled intention is a condemnation[1] of the manner of living represented by these Parisians. The keynotes here are drabness and monotony, seen immediately in the scenes of the Ralon and the Mogne families that alternate in section 1. The sordid, trash-littered courtyard surveyed by Jean Ralon on the first page provides an objective correlative for the empty ennui of humdrum lives. The Vertigues, despite their greater wealth, are trapped in the petty social competition of their class. By occupying their minds in superficial routines, these individuals avoid unsettling truths. Jean Ralon will not, in his waking hours, confront his crumbling religious faith, nor will his brother Alexis face his homosexual attraction to their nephew, Louis Lécuyer. Their mother, Virginie Ralon, refuses to admit that her servant was her husband's lover. The residents can acknowledge Samuel Léonard's ambiguous relations with his homosexual houseboy and his "niece" (actually his illegitimate daughter) only by means of anti-Semitic innuendos.

Beneath this monotony and bad faith lies a deep alienation. This is not a portrait of life in an apartment building but of life on five separate floors whose residents scarcely communicate. This evening might seem an exception since members of most of the building's households have been invited to Angèle Vertigues's birthday celebration. It is soon clear, however, that there will be no interpenetration; the party becomes, in fact, an occasion to reinforce existing relationships and to remind each participant of his status in the preordained hierarchy. Louis Lécuyer and Henriette Ledu are both treated as outcasts: he as the priests' penniless nephew and she as Léonard's illegitimate Jewish daughter. M. Vertigues attempts to keep the importunate Henri Delétang at the distance appropriate to a social inferior and is in turn the object of the scorn of the snobbish Philippe Sermaize. The barriers are, however, vertical as well as horizontal: there is scarcely more communication between residents within the same apartment than between those in different apartments. Alexis and Jean Ralon both complain to themselves that they cannot talk to each other, and neither communicates with their mother. The Mogne household, the largest in the building, is paradoxically the loneliest. Henri, the son-in-law, is only barely tolerated, and Paul Mogne and Marie Mérédat, Frédéric's elderly in-laws, are treated with indifferent neglect by the younger members.

The boredom and alienation reflect deeper social problems. These people do not constitute a community, a cultural unit; they are simply an aggregate of human beings, a crowd. They lack a coherent system of shared beliefs or ideals which might unify and energize their lives. The nominal commitment to Catholicism, reflected in the presence of the two priests, appears to have no further impact in the lives of the building's inhabitants than the anti-Semitism directed against the Léonards by the Ralons, the Mognes, and the concierge. The building stands, symbolically, over the crypt of an ancient church, long forgotten like the religion of which it is a relic.

In emphasizing the drab lives of these bored Parisians, we have neglected one very significant flash of exotic color. Jean Ralon on the first floor and Samuel Léonard on the third are both Egyptologists. The latter has filled his apartment with oriental antiquities and has brought with him his Egyptian servant and lover, Ahmed. The building is thus suffused with a faint but distinctive Egyptian coloration. The novel's principal narrative movement is to merge the worlds of Paris and Egypt, both in the characters' conscious and in their unconscious lives. The building's Christian residents are drawn into contact with the "Egyptians" (Samuel Léonard, his daughter Henriette Ledu, and his servant Ahmed), whom they have shunned because of racial, religious, and sexual prejudices. There is an initial, superficial contact at the birthday party. Louis reluctantly escorts Henriette, and Léonard sends Ahmed to help serve at the party. Angèle's accidental death at Louis Lécuyer's hands, however, draws the entire building together around Léonard in a conspiracy to prevent scandal and save Louis by sending him to Egypt. It is significant of the temporary unification of the residents that Louis Lécuyer, in the chain of events preceding and following Angèle's death, goes from the sixth floor to the first, to the fourth, to the roof, to the basement, to the third, and finally to the first again. The novel ends with a Parisian's "conversion": Louis will begin life anew under Léonard's tutelage in Egypt.

These Parisians also encounter Egypt on deep psychological and symbolic levels. In the early morning hours preceding the killing, Jean Ralon dreams of sailing down a subterranean river on a boat directed by an Egyptian servant resembling Ahmed (206). These dreams, as Jennifer Waelti-Walters[2] has shown, are profoundly shaped by the priest's reading of the Egyptian *Book of the Dead*. Ralon travels the mythical river Tuat toward the Judgment Hall where he will face Osiris. Upon arrival, however, he is denied admittance. When he clutches his rosary and prays to the Blessed Virgin, he finds that these gestures avail him nothing. After awakening, he realizes that he has missed the key moment in the ritual (282–83). Professor Waelti-

Walters has identified this moment as the instant when the night-sun god Af is transformed into the day-sun god Shu, causing the rebirth of all the blessed souls.

Jean Ralon's underground voyage as well as his fears of divine abandonment are anticipated by a Latin passage that he reads earlier in his breviary:

> Because my soul is filled with evil and my life cast into hell.
> I am looked upon as one cast into the pit, I have become as a man without help among the dead.
> I am like those slaughtered, who sleep in graves and who are no longer remembered, and they are cast out by your very own hands.
> They have put me into the very deep pit in darkness and in the shadow of death. (162)

The text is Psalm 87, part of the matins liturgy for Good Friday, which places Jean Ralon's descent in Holy Week[3] at the time of Christ's descent into Hell. And yet this Catholic priest's dreams assume not Christian but "pagan," Egyptian forms. This fact, rendered psychologically plausible by Ralon's study of ancient beliefs, reveals the profound religious disorder in which he lives.

The priest's Egyptian studies have clearly had a corrosive effect on his Christian faith. Butor has detected echoes of the *Book of the Dead* in the Coptic Christian liturgy[4] and noted the Old Testament's assimilation of ancient Egyptian maxims. He describes his reaction to the latter discovery: "It was a ray of light on my origins and on those of the religion in which I had been raised."[5] The modern Christian smugly assumes religious superiority based on a unique revelation passing through Judaism to Christianity; however, the discovery of his faith's debt to a supposedly inferior, "heathen" religion subtly undercuts this assumption. On a more general level, Jean Ralon, like Butor himself, must surely have been impressed by the ancient Egyptian's religious genius, and this recognition must have further weakened his Christian faith. Ralon tries to suppress these doubts, but Egypt's "beautiful demons . . . take advantage of nocturnal openings"[6] and invade his dreams. At the same time, he cannot release his crucifix and enter fully into the Egyptian world: he is trapped between two realms, unable to go back or move ahead. Alexis Ralon's dreams repeat certain motifs of those of his brother: he also sails through the dark in a boat (211) and unsuccessfully implores his Christian god for aid (196–97). In this case, the repressed fear he must face is his sexual attraction for Louis. It is, however, Louis who completes the mythic voyage begun by his uncles. He dreams of ripping away the Blessed Virgin's veil and discovering the face of a cat (264), symbol of Bast, Egyptian goddess of love. He is thus granted the face-to-face confrontation with the divinity denied his uncle Jean.

These symbolic journeys run parallel to literal journeys and eruptions from the underworld. The novel's climactic events, Henri Delétang's attempted kidnap of Angèle Vertigues and her accidental death at the hands of Louis Lécuyer, occur in the early morning hours while most of the building's residents are asleep. Henri and Louis both wander in an underground passage, the building's cave, whose dank atmosphere (266, 268) recalls the world of Jean Ralon's nightmare. Louis, like his uncle, meets an "Egyptian," Samuel Léonard, and the two move as in a dream (268). Henri and Louis, who come up from the underground to interrupt the sleep of the building's residents, represent that which is repressed both socially and psychologically in their awakened life. They are its social outcasts: Henri, for obscure reasons related to his father's business relationship with M. Vertigues, and Louis as an impoverished and fatherless child. They carry within themselves emotions they are prevented from expressing openly. It is Henri's resentment of the Vertigues and Louis's thwarted love of their daughter that draw them to the fourth floor after the party has ended, thus releasing the tragic chain of events that climaxes the novel. This explosion from the underworld, both in the night's actions and in its dreams, is prefigured by the subway's premonitory rumblings beneath the building (13, 35, 56, 73, 99, 135). Explicit references in the text invite us to see this underground journey and the death of this young virgin in terms of a primitive ritual. At the party, Louis expresses a desire to follow "that very knowledgeable ceremony, that appears linked to very basic and long-forgotten primitive beliefs,"[7] and after the death of Angèle he sees himself and the others as "actors in a liturgical drama."[8] Butor was even more direct in describing the party to an interviewer: "It is a feast of passage from youth to adulthood. It is, in a sense, our society's equivalent, our society's shadow, of the initiation celebration. This bringing together of all the elements, all the individuals living within the same building provokes, not only the awareness for each individual of other individuals, but also of a certain number of common elements which linger in their consciousness."[9]

Rites of passage seek to produce a second birth, regeneration at another level. We need, therefore, to clarify the nature and terms of the transfer which take place in Louis's case. Angèle Vertigues is, as her name suggests, the "angel of the heights" who presides over the world represented by this building. The adored daughter of its most important family, it is she to whom all pay obeisance on this night. A suitor describes her as a "protective divinity,"[10] and Louis sees her in his dream dressed as the Blessed Virgin (263). She is, then, the symbolic center of the building's prevailing Christian, bourgeois moral and social order. Louis kills Angèle, and Bast, the Egyptian goddess of love, replaces her in his dreams (264). Aided by Léonard, Louis emerges into the morning light to depart for a new life in Egypt. Butor's first novel, like his autobiographical *Portrait d'artiste en jeune singe*, ends with a flight into Egypt; Louis's departure leads, we assume, to the same "second birth"[11] experienced by Butor.

Butor deliberately uses references to the world he discovered in the Nile Valley as "a kind of sounding box, a sort of reference, a point of comparison."[12] His discussion of Egypt in other writings illuminates this important theme in *Passage de Milan*. Egypt functions in the novel as a contrasting surface against which the peculiar features of contemporary Western society can better be seen. Butor found, as Herodotus had many years earlier, that Egyptians differ strikingly from Europeans. He attributes their unique world view to their dramatic geographical situation. Extraordinary parallel cliffs rise abruptly on each side of the Nile, dividing the country into two radically different regions. The banks of the Nile are rich and fertile with the deposits of many floodings. This heavily cultivated area is the center of population and activity. Beyond the cliffs, however, another hostile universe manifests itself: "a space where we were nothing, like the soil of another planet . . . the rock worn by the wind, the globe's dry bark."[13] The desert wasteland's menacing power is a continuing theme in Butor's descriptions of Egypt: in a poem it becomes the "prairie of the gods' fury,"[14] and we are told in a radio play that "the sunrise in Egypt does not have the lovely vermillion tints that one admires in the Cyclades or on the Candian coast; the sun suddenly explodes on the horizon, preceded only by a vague white light, it sometimes seems to slowly lift the long folds of a grey shroud, and appears pale to us and without light, like Osiris underground."[15]

Egypt's brutal terrain inevitably reminds us of Camus's Algeria: the same pitiless sun, the same empty wasteland. This landscape produces in Butor a recognition very like that feeling of absurdity experienced by Camus. The European's facile and romantic idealization of nature is quite impossible: man finds himself in the presence of a powerful and vaguely hostile force. Even within the fertile areas, the constant changes of the Nile menace all landmarks: "everything appears ephemeral, the men and domestic animals of course, but also the very shape of the terrain."[16] This harsh environment produces in the Nile Valley's inhabitants a "constant awareness of the individual's transitory existence, so different from the kind of forgetfulness of this condition that now prevails in most Western European countries."[17] Granted this awareness, the value of Egypt as a point of comparison becomes clear. This profound, stoic recognition of life's ephemerality contrasts starkly with the Parisians' triviality and self-deception.

And yet it is not merely the Egyptians' awareness of death that makes them unique; they have situated this awareness within an integrated, total view of the world. Their environment compounded of opposites—the extremely fertile Nile and the forbidding moonscape which rises a few hundred yards from the river—the Egyptians must fuse the different poles of existence: "the organization of their society, to be stable, had itself to integrate a contrast, be founded on an equilibrium of opposites."[18] We have seen Butor's emphasis on structures which will encompass all of our experience; thus the Egyptians' success in this area must be counted one of the principal sources of Butor's interest in this civilization. The pharoah Min first unified upper and lower Egypt and became synonymous in Egyptian myth with cultural unity. Min's symbol, we learn in *Degrés* (*10*, 12) is the *milan*, or kite, suggesting another connotation for the bird that appears in the title of Butor's first novel. Louis Lécuyer's underground journey leads to a new life in a culture which is the direct opposite of the discredited world he leaves behind. For those of us who identify with his voyage but who remain behind in Europe or North America it also has a function. Egypt offers us a point of contrast by means of which we can criticize our world, a place from which we can balance our lever as we attempt to change it. We emerge, blinking with Louis in the morning light, our eyes cleansed, better able to understand and transform our own lives.

But what of those left behind, those who refuse the journey's lessons? Jean Ralon, the character with whom the novel opens and closes, is an extremely important negative illustration of Butor's thesis about our relationship with the past. Although a student of history, Jean Ralon steadfastly resists the implications of his knowledge. Significantly, he is refused admittance to the Judgment Hall which leads to rebirth. We last see him fearing his altar boy's glances as he prepares to worship at the Catholic altar in which he no longer believes but which he cannot renounce. The consequences can only be continued bad faith, confusion, and nightmares. "Every head," Butor explains in his novel, "is a warehouse where statues of gods and demons of every size and age sleep, whose inventory is never completed."[19] We must recognize these buried divinities not simply out of an obscurantist's interest in ancient history but because they represent ways of living, once realized in the past, that are different from our present modes. To ignore these ancient cultures is to evade the important human needs to which they were a response. These "gods" and the instincts they symbolized can be repressed only temporarily; then they return, "laughing at us from in hiding, feeding on our mental reservations."[20]

Jean Ralon's refusal of the past is not unique; a survey of other modern reactions to ancient Egypt clarifies a problem confronted by many of Butor's characters. The Nile Valley's contemporary Muslims live in the presence of imposing but dimly understood relics of the ancient world. These intimidating monuments are testimony to the greatness achieved by a culture different from their own. The modern Egyptian, in his ignorance, projects his fears and superstitions on these relics, making them "a dark and dangerous background . . . haunted by strange lights."[21] To exorcise these fears and demonstrate their own religious superiority, the Muslims incorporated stones from ancient monuments into their own more recent structures. Thus in entering the Khanquah of Sultan Beebars one must tread on carvings from the period of Ramses X.[22] No less a civilization than Imperial Rome experienced this same anxious need to bring back obelisks to decorate its city and demonstrate its own superiority. So also with the French Empire: Napoleon imported the obelisk that adorns the Place de la Concorde.[23] Butor has sprinkled his works with examples of the French fascination with Egypt which followed Napoleon's return from the Nile: he describes the curious Egyptian house at 2 Place du Caire, the porch of the hotel Beauharnais, and the Fontaine du Fellah.[24] The French Empire's "Egyptian" motifs, like Rome's obelisk, are the conqueror's gesture toward a subject culture rather than the archeologist's serious attempt to understand or assimilate Egypt's lesson. Western Europe remains smug in its ascendancy; history begins with the Greeks and remains wholly European until the torch, very recently and very reluctantly, is passed to North America. Thus "groups as large and prestigious as Egyptian antiquity or Islam figure in this representation only as appendices, footnotes, amusing vignettes."[25]

Without a proper understanding, ancient Egypt inevitably remains a vaguely menacing presence associated with strange "pagan" and superstitious practices. But this ignorance and fear need not exist; *Degrés'* young students are genuinely excited by their studies of ancient Egypt. Their teacher watches "their eyes open, the longing to travel spread from head to head, like fire from tree to tree in a dry forest."[26] Butor cites Bossuet's belief that Egypt could be a source of inspiration greater than Greece and Rome[27] and recalls Rabelais's dreams of recovering the ancient Egyptian learning which would be the "model of a future language, utopia."[28]

Here we come to an idea that is absolutely central to Butor's historical explorations: it is, paradoxically, the descent into the past that opens the future. Freed from the limiting perspective of the present we discover new ways of thinking and living that we can use as we plan tomorrow. *Passage de Milan* discusses the future; one of its subplots is the futurological speculations of the group gathered around Samuel Léonard. We will have more to say about such speculations in a later chapter; for the present it is important to note that Butor structures his novel in such a manner that the descent into the mythic past and the discussion of the future occur simultaneously. The novel's central section, Chapter 7, covering the first hour after midnight, consists primarily of an alternation of Jean Ralon's Egyptian dreams and the Léonard group's futurological conversations. These alternating scenes complement one another. One of the amateur futurologists proposes that the study of the future replace entirely the study of the past (165), but a colleague perceptively wonders how we would recognize this future as our own without a knowledge of our past (181). The past cannot be forgotten we are told; our plans for the future would inevitably be infiltrated by "ancient powers, ancient desires . . . ancient fears."[29]

This book's clear implication, both in its structure and in its themes, is that the recovery of the past and the planning of the future must proceed hand in hand. Samuel Léonard, Louis Lécuyer's guide, is both an archeologist and a futurologist; Egypt, the land toward which they travel, is both our past and Louis's new future.

At the time of its publication in 1954, *Passage de Milan* passed virtually unnoticed. After the success of Butor's subsequent books, however, critics have carefully analyzed his first novel, and the Collection 10/18 has issued an inexpensive paperback edition. Clearly, familiarity with the later works has taught us how to read this beginning effort. Here are the basic themes we will meet again and again: the poverty of modern society and the contrasting richness of an ancient culture. But comparison with later works also reveals *Passage de Milan*'s weaknesses. The Egyptian cultural background remains too obscure, and the novel's focus is too diffuse. Narrative point of view shifts disconcertingly from authorial omniscience to the private views of dozens of characters. The reader cannot easily understand or identify with the problems besetting any one of the characters. Butor learned from this first effort and, as we shall see in his second novel, soon found more successful ways of dramatizing his cultural themes and managing the reader's perspective.

CHAPTER 2

L'Emploi du temps

Butor's second novel, *L'Emploi du temps*, considerably expands his historical schema, uncovering a whole series of earlier cultures buried within a modern industrial city. Jacques Revel, the novel's protagonist, has come to spend a year working as a commercial translator in Bleston, a mythical northern British city. Butor, drawing on his own impressions of Manchester, paints a depressing portrait of this area —sooty air, grimy buildings, and interminably drizzling skies.[1] Drugged by this environment, Revel discovers after seven months that he has slipped into a mindless stupor; he can neither remember his past nor explain his present actions. Revel blames these behavioral changes on Bleston's strange power over his consciousness (*27, 31*). He decides to combat the effects of this place by writing a journal which will reconstruct the time he has spent in Bleston and explain what has happened to him. Revel's struggle to resist this industrial metropolis is offered by Butor not as the story of an isolated individual but as an example of man's plight in today's society. Bleston, Revel realizes, is the synthesis of the problems of many blighted modern cities: "Bleston is not unique . . . Manchester, or Leeds, Newcastle or Sheffield or Liverpool . . . or else, no doubt, some modern American town such as Pittsburgh or Detroit, would have had a similar effect on me."[2] Britain's dreary, polluted northern cities, Butor feels, can teach us "something very important on what industrial cities are as a whole, and thus on contemporary Western civilization."[3]

Revel frequently describes his exploration of Bleston and our modern culture in terms suggesting an archeological excavation: he refers to his work several times as a "fouille" or dig (*84, 197, 223*; 83, 189, 223) and says, "I suddenly stumble at the edge of a cleft at the bottom of which the original soil is laid bare, and thus I can gauge the thickness of the silt which I must plumb and filter in order to recover my bedrock, my foundations."[4] This archeological metaphor focuses our attention on the novel's central purposes. Butor is, first of all, interested in exploring, not just the year of a Frenchman in a modern city, but also the cultural forces that lie buried within that city and our civilization. Moreover, Butor and Revel explore the city much as an archeologist might, by examining its principal artistic and architectural monuments. It is significant that the two most important works of art in Revel's investigation, the Museum of Fine Arts' Harrey tapestries and the Old Cathedral's windows, were both created in Revel's native France, from which he feels separated by a "huge gulf."[5] We shall see how his study of these works of art helps him restore his contact with the roots of his own continental culture.

Revel discovers in the Theseus myth portrayed in the eighteenth-century Harrey tapestries important analogies to his own situation. He sees the Bailey sisters, two young Blestonians who befriend and aid him, as Ariadne and Phaedra, and himself as Theseus. Like Theseus on Crete, Revel is a stranger on a foreign island whose romantic attentions shift from one sister (Ann Bailey-Ariadne) to the other (Rose Bailey-Phaedra). He also sees his attempt to decipher Bleston's secrets and break its power over his life as similar to Theseus' attempt to penetrate the labyrinth and break the Minotaur's power over Athens. His journal is thus "an Ariadne's thread"[6] which will enable him to penetrate the city's mysterious heart.

Jacques Revel is drawn to the Theseus myth both by the analogies with his own situation and because it establishes a link with the warm, sensual world of the Mediterranean, whose beaches are "perpetually glistening under the salt kiss of the blue water."[7] We have already seen Butor's use of Egypt's bright deserts as a contrast to Paris's drab apartments; the sunny, sensuous Greek world performs a similar function in this novel. During one of his reveries on Ariadne and Phaedra, Revel contrasts the overt sensuality of their world with cold and repressive Bleston: "Ariadne and Phaedra . . . with huge eyes and slender waists . . . and with breasts exposed in low-cut, close-fitting bodices, breasts like tender peaches, such as I imagine Rose's to be (every lovely face or form irresistibly takes me back to hers) under her high-necked sweater."[8] This erotic dimension is crucial to the nostalgia for ancient Mediterranean cultures that suffuses many of Butor's works. He praises "antiquity's *frankness* in its considera-tion of the human body"[9] and contrasts this attitude to that of puri-tanical and repressive Christianity.

The Christian gazes steadfastly heavenward, refusing this world, but the ancient Greek accepted and celebrated man's fleshly exis-tence: "ancient religion, far from prohibiting our gaze, managed to illuminate it; Homer's brilliant vision or the sculptor's . . . transformed nature's spectacle for all of society."[10]

More important than the analogies between Revel and Theseus are the ironic contrasts; despite similarities in their situations, Revel's world is not Theseus', and it is modern industrial society which suffers by the contrast. The Harrey tapestries, suggesting Greek beauty and sensuality, hang ignored and seldom visited in Bleston Museum's dark galleries. A Greek vase, some Roman coins, and a sarcophagus constitute the museum's entire collection of classical antiquities. The museum building, constructed in the Greek Revival style, its Ionic columns stained by Bleston's soot (68, 69), symbolizes the degraded and disfigured manner in which Greek civilization survives in Bleston. Butor describes the Greek Revival style as "a complete misunderstanding of Greece—these insufferable buildings cause, in their pretentious vulgarity, a feeling of profound historical discontinuity."[11] The Blestonians' ignorance of their own classical roots is such that they believe the town's name to be derived from the English "Bells Town" rather than from its true Latin etymology "Belli Civitas."

Revel's "archeological" explorations lead him to another mythical figure: the Bible's Cain, enshrined in the Old Cathedral's windows. The young Frenchman is surprised to discover the legendary fratricide occupying a place of honor in a Christian church. His priest-guide explains, however, that the Renaissance regarded Cain as the "father of all the arts."[12] This notion has as its source no less an authority than chapter 4 of *Genesis*. The window's sixteenth-century creators, following this text, portray Cain as the founder of the first city, which they have modeled on the Bleston of their day. Revel's guide describes its population of artists and artisans. There are Cain's sons: Yabal, father of those who spin, dye, and sew; Tubal Cain, leader of those who work with metal; and Yubal, the first musician, surrounded by his many wind and stringed instruments. Intrigued by the contrast between Renaissance Bleston and modern Bleston, Revel asks, "Bleston, city of weavers and metal workers, what has become of your musicians?"[13] The only answer is a heavy truck's dull rumble. The clear implication is that although the Renaissance city included a place for the artist, its modern British counterpart has banished him in its exclusive emphasis on the textile and steel industries.

The respect in which the Renaissance held Cain was a momentary aberration in the Judeo-Christian religious tradition, which has usually treated him as a villainous outcast. Butor returned to Cain in his 1971 Beethoven *Dialogues*, which incorporates Gérard de Nerval's legend of Adoniram, Solomon's chief architect and a descendant of Cain.

Adoniram journeys underground to meet his famous ancestor. He learns that Jehovah condemned Cain for offering civilization to man, challenging the Jewish god's tyrannical hegemony. Adoniram also learns of his own descendants' eventual triumph over Jehovah and the inauguration of a new reign of freedom. Cain symbolizes, both for Nerval and Butor, the artist's revolt against the prevailing order. Cain, in fact, in many ways resembles Theseus: both killed, breaking the power of an earlier order, and became leaders of great cities (71, 72). Revel, because of his deliberate assault on Bleston and his inadvertent attack on certain of its citizens, becomes himself a son of Cain, his hands stained by the blood streaming from Cain's window (205, 197).

A place for Cain must be found in our society. Jean Roudaut, citing Saint Augustine, reminds us that Cain is the founder of the City of Man. To reject Cain is to reject humanism and create a dangerous gulf between the secular and the sacred.[14] The Old Cathedral's architects originally conceived two series of windows: a group portraying the secular cities flowing from Cain and another group of holy cities flowing from Abel. They intended that both groups be viewed together as part of a vast scheme climaxing in the celestial Jerusalem at the end of history (76, 77). The cathedral windows would have traced Bleston's origins back in time and plotted its course into the future. The Reformation intervened, however, and the culminating New Jerusalem window was never finished. Without this scene orienting the future, the ancient cities are confused and seen "the wrong way round."[15] Future and past are inextricably linked; to change or destroy one inevitably changes the other as well. The reformers compounded this confusion. Repudiating a church grown worldly, they swung to the other extreme and utterly rejected the secular. Rioting schismatics removed Abel's windows from the cathedral, leaving the Cain windows isolated in the hated Roman Catholic citadel. Destroying a tradition which saw man's creatural and spiritual natures as parts of a balanced whole produced an effect opposite to that intended by Bleston's Reformers. Radically separating the human and the divine, far from purifying and elevating Bleston, left it with no models but those of the profane cities. The sulphurous rain which falls on Sodom in one of the extant windows continues to fall on modern Bleston (76, 262; 78, 252), and the depiction of the Tower of Babel in another window is echoed in the construction of Bleston's massive new department store (76, 240; 78, 230).

The windows also reveal the ambiguous and often hostile relations between the Judeo-Christian tradition and classical civilization. The

Cathedral architect represented classical Rome among the cities of Cain, as the priest-guide explains to Revel:

> "Yes, Rome the Imperial City; opposite on the other side, on the left of the choir from where we stand, but on the right hand of Christ the Judge in the big east window, was Rome the Papal City, the Capital of the Church."
> "Is nothing left of it?"
> "Absolutely nothing is left of any of the windows on the other side."
> The explanation he gave me, far from solving the mystery, only sharpened and deepened it. There was a strange ambiguity about the way the old-time glaziers had set out their subjects, as if wishing to show through their illustration of the official Biblical text that they themselves had read something else into it.[16]

The disposition of these windows is pregnant with meaning. Already implicit in medieval and Renaissance Christianity was a tendency to consider the classical world as unholy and to insist on a radical cleavage between Christianity and pagan antiquity. Yet at the same time there was also a desire to adapt and transform classical forms and ideas to Christian purposes. The Renaissance popes assiduously collected classical art as models for the Christian artists they sponsored; thus Revel discovers classical civilization "enclosed in the labyrinth of the popes."[17] Unfortunately, the Blestonians destroyed the window depicting papal Rome, an act symbolic of the Anglican schism, and they are without even the secondary and somewhat transformed contact with classical civilization which Renaissance and baroque Rome might have provided.

Christianity is, for Butor, our greatest source of cultural discord. "The war between two systems of contradictory values, two traditions, the 'Christian' and the 'classical' "[18] has had the gravest consequences for Europe and is a theme to which Butor will return in much greater detail in *La Modification*. Here in this novel, it is significant that both of the city's principal artistic treasures, the tapestries and the windows, portray killers: Theseus, slayer of the minotaur and inadvertant cause of his father's death, and Cain, the fratricide. They are "two great hieroglyphs that set the mark of the murderer on Bleston's brow, on the brow of that city haunted by murder."[19] The river dividing the city is called the Slee (its French pronunciation would approximate the English "slay"); the town's Latin name means City of War; and the Old Cathedral is built on the site of the Roman military temple. Strife and murder permeate this city torn by competing traditions. The struggles of Christianity versus classicism and

Protestantism versus Catholicism have sown bitterness and destroyed important parts of the cultural patrimony.

The Old Cathedral fell into general disuse after the Protestants built the New Cathedral during the mid-nineteenth century. This latter edifice features an unusual system of decoration inspired by the natural sciences, which were expanding during the period of its construction. In decorating the New Cathedral, its designers attempted to illustrate all the zoological phyla and botanical classes, as well as many minerals. The church is thus a kind of evolutionary museum with space devoted to each group: plants in the side aisles, invertebrates in the nave, and the human races in the choir. The goal is a synthesizing vision of man and his evolutionary past. Revel, impressed by the Old Cathedral and influenced by his friend George Burton, is initially repelled by the New Cathedral. Gradually, however, he becomes strangely fascinated by this building and recognizes "a mind of astonishing audacity at work, violently distorting traditional themes, ornaments and details, achieving thus an imperfect, one might almost say a crippled, work of art, but a profoundly imaginative one, with a secret seminal force, poignantly striving toward freer and happier creation."[20]

The most audacious and successful attempt to integrate natural forms into ecclesiastical architecture—and Butor's source for the New Cathedral—is Antonio Gaudí's Sagrada Familia church, which Butor visited in Barcelona while working on this novel.[21] Gaudí incorporated numerous animals and plants (turtles, sea birds, snails, and so forth) in his extraordinary decorative scheme. Butor has written appreciatively of Gaudí, who resolved the tension between the modern age's scientific interests and its outmoded architectural decoration. The rigid adherence to decorative schemes borrowed from an earlier era, the Neogothic for example, produced a profound discrepancy between the society's true interests and its principal architectural monuments. Gaudí attempted to integrate his church into the contemporary world by borrowing his decorative scheme from the natural sciences: "Envisioning the forms of his time within what I would call a 'complete architectural space,' that is, linking his constructions to all aspects of the society within which he was realizing them, Gaudí was able to deliver them from their internal contradictions, and endow them, in relation to their contradictions, with an extraordinary innovative value whose fruits we enjoy today."[22] Although it is never explicitly stated, Revel's enthusiasm for the New Cathedral seems motivated by a similar recognition of an audacious new architectural style which might unite the many disparate elements of modern civilization. Gaudí's church was, unfortunately, never completed and is today ignored by many Spaniards. Similarly, the New Cathedral is misunderstood and little visited by Blestonians.

On one of his last days in the city, Revel notices the construction of a new department store which will obscure much of the New Cathedral and realizes how contemporary commercialism distracts us from genuine artistic achievement: "that sunlit facade so loudly proclaiming its newness made me almost forget the older building which I had meant to visit once again . . . because I could not help seeing through the tall colorless windows that huge wall of gleaming bricks, too sure a proof of the evil city's vitality, a token of change canceling all hope of genuine change."[23] The department store is not the only product of modern commercialism that distracts Blestonians. Plaisance Gardens, a tawdry amusement park, attracts large crowds and is appropriately compared by Revel to the anticathedral which dominates Cain's city in the windows (*147*, 141). Revel discovers the same cynical escapism at the cinema. Historical superproductions, such as "Red Nights of Roma" (see *238*, 228) simultaneously exploit modern man's desire to escape an oppressive present and deceive him about the true nature of the past.

Revel's patient exploration of Bleston, its buildings, and its art enables him to discover the way important parts of our classical, Judeo-Christian, and even modern cultures have been misunderstood, destroyed, or ignored. His search bears fruit late in the novel on 27 August when, in a lyrical passage spanning four pages, he envisions a series of ancient and modern cities. He is thus able to reconstruct the historical tradition of which Bleston is a part; the new consciousness gives Revel courage to face the future:

> into my vision of Rome there intruded not only the images of conquered Athens, of Petra, Baalbeck and Timgad, but also that of Bleston, city of doom and oblivion, the ancient town of Bleston, Bellista, Belli Civitas, cause of my misery . . .
> and at the same moment I saw the town itself in a new light, as though the wall alongside which I have been groping ever since my arrival, here and there less opaque, had suddenly grown thinner, disclosing forgotten depths, so that my shrinking courage returned and I felt once again, thanks to this unfamiliar light, capable of defying the town and protecting myself from it, of resisting it more strongly.[24]

L'Emploi du temps discusses not only the contents of our past but the way in which this past can be explored. The French title refers, first, to the *schedule* or the organization of Revel's time; it also refers to the *use* of time, the way which the past can be employed to illuminate the present and orient the future. In his effort to organize and understand his past, Revel studies and rejects several models. His first initiatory guide in Bleston is Horace Buck, an African laborer. Like the lonely refugee from India who wanders through another of Butor's British texts,[25] Buck is the hapless victim of capitalist imperialism, which first subjugated his homeland and then imported him as cheap labor. Buck rebels against his own entrapment by drunkenness and pyromania. Revel is tempted and momentarily succumbs to this response; he burns his map of Bleston, effigy of the city. He soon repudiates such an irrational action, however, and eventually transforms these destructive flames into the light (3, 9) cast by his journal.

Revel's second guide, the detective novelist George Burton, aids Revel's literary efforts. The young Frenchman is immediately attracted to Burton's *The Bleston Murder* (*Le Meurtre de Bleston*), a novel whose title ambiguously refers both to a murder committed *in* Bleston and to the murder *of* Bleston (Revel's deepest desire). Since coming to Bleston and prior to discovering Burton's novel, Revel, normally a voracious reader, has read virtually nothing and suffers the numbing effects of this deprivation (54, 55–56). Revel's discovery of Burton's novel returns him to his old habits and consoles him with the knowledge that another shares his hatred of the city. The novel and its author also provide him with a structure for organizing his own inquiry. Burton explains to Revel that the detective is one who "kills" or explodes the mystery and confusion created by the initial crime (152–54, 146–48). The crime Revel wishes to expose is Bleston's murder of his consciousness, and he finds the detective story structure ideally suited to his purpose. The detective reorders events spatially, forcing a revelation from them. His narrative actually superimposes two separate narrative sequences: the events leading up to the murder and the inquest following the crime (179, 171). Revel's journal in its initial stages is based on this same pattern; it consists of the events since his arrival leading up to his irrational acts in late April and the events concurrent with his writing beginning in May.

Unfortunately, George Burton, like Horace Buck, proves only temporarily useful; his weapon, the detective novel, turns out to be a faulty instrument. The murder mystery leads to facile, closed solutions: guilt is always located in a single individual or conspiracy which is then isolated and eliminated. Burton's analysis of Bleston is clear and unequivocal: the New Cathedral and the modern world it represents are the source of all the city's troubles. Revel discovers, however, that the New Cathedral was a richly promising effort. He gradually realizes that Bleston's problems are much more complex than Burton allows, and so he becomes disillusioned with Burton and his detective structure. The detective writer's model of our relationship to the past and his juxtaposition of two time schemes are simplistic and inadequate solutions. Our perspective on the past changes as events occur in the present, causing a reevaluation of what we had previously discovered. Revel adds three more sequences, two moving backward and one forward, to his narrative schema. The result is five levels of past time, in addition to the time of narration.

This multi-leveled view of the past enables Revel to see events in the context of a whole series of anterior and posterior occurrences. We see this approach in action in the journal entries preceding the climactic vision of 27 August. His journal entry of 25 August recalls his recent viewing of travelogues on Athens (25 August) and Rome (18 August). On the twenty-fifth he also reread his journal entries for late June, when he saw a travelogue on Petra (16 June), and recorded his study of the New Cathedral on 18 November, a visit which cast interesting retrospective light on his visit to the Old Cathedral (4 November). On 27 August he recalls his visit to the remains of Roman Bleston in the museum. Many separate personal and cultural experiences in June, August, and November are thus juxtaposed, influencing one another and triggering other memories. When Revel begins on 27 August to describe the images of imperial Rome recently projected at the cinema, images of a whole series of other cities intervene, leading to that moment of historical revelation described earlier. Numerous ancient and modern cities, isolated in history and seen separately by Revel, are viewed simultaneously as part of a single culture culminating in modern Bleston. It is precisely because Revel has forsworn a simple, linear, temporal perspective that he is able to grasp the significance of many, seemingly unconnected discoveries during his Bleston year.

Revel describes his elaborate temporal structure both as an immense scaffolding protecting his archeological excavation and as an observatory (*299*, 289) from which he can see the individual event's significance. This tower is also, however, a vantage point for surveying the future. After his relentless pursuit of the forces buried within Bleston, Revel gradually realizes that the city secretly wants his work to continue and succeed. His journal changes, in its final pages, from a personal record into an open letter to the Bailey sisters, and beyond them, to the entire city, inviting their involvement in a continuing quest (*278*, 268).

Unlike the detective novelist who solves his mystery, calming our anxieties, Revel and Butor deliberately leave their work unsettlingly open. Revel cannot complete his narrative, and key dates which are left unexplained form a kind of "question mark."[26] Even if additional time for narration were added, further levels of the past would surely be discovered. Revel's archeological excavation remains incomplete: he regrets, as time runs out, his failure to explore a promising area containing St. Jude's church, with another group of windows, and a synagogue (273, 263). We can only wonder what new discoveries might have been made at these additional sites. The unfinished journal reminds us of the function of the incomplete or open work: "since the work should be indefinitely continued by its readers, in particular those who will themselves write others more or less clearly related to it, it should offer itself as unfinished, not the circle to which one can add nothing, but the spiral which invites our pursuit."[27]

Our relationship to the past and responsibility for the present are in *L'Emploi du temps* conceived in terms considerably more complex than those of *Passage de Milan*. Louis Lécuyer's liberation from the apartment building and his new beginnings in Egypt are bestowed on him accidentally. To be sure, the simultaneous parallels between his real voyage and his uncle's imagined voyages suggest a relationship between their failures and his success; but his escape occurs, nonetheless, through no conscious effort of his own toward freedom. Jacques Revel's movement toward understanding results, however, from his own dogged probing of his and Bleston's past. The limited point of view and long, tortuous sentences of *L'Emploi du temps* join our minds to Revel's, forcing us to experience his laborious struggle for consciousness. The tools to understand the past and direct the future are placed in our own hands.

Passage de Milan concerns itself almost exclusively with the Egyptian past; the past of *L'Emploi du temps* is much more richly layered. Butor skillfully uses imaginary works of art to dramatize a whole series of cultural levels. Seen retrospectively through the lens of the second novel, Louis Lécuyer's landing in the Nile Delta can only be the beginning of a long education and not its conclusion. *L'Emploi du temps* disabuses us of any hope for simple solutions: there are no single guides, either mythic (Theseus, Cain), artistic (the Old Cathedral, the New Cathedral), or human (Horace Buck, George Burton). "Any gospel that is taken as the gospel is apocryphal."[28] There is, moreover, no single historical golden age into which we can retreat; Butor's next novel, as we shall see, specifically denounces such an attempt at historical self-deception.

CHAPTER 3

La Modification

While exploring Bleston's Old Cathedral, Jacques Revel discovers two significant and provocative windows portraying two versions of Rome. Butor's third novel, *La Modification*, might be taken as a reconstruction and an enlargement of these windows and their themes: the relations between classical and Christian Rome.

The novel recounts the train journey of Léon Delmont, a Parisian businessman en route to Rome, where he plans to join his mistress, Cécile Darcella. The trip is, he believes, the most important in his life, for by it he means to break completely with his Parisian life and begin a new one in Rome with his true love. Although Delmont's job places him at a higher economic and social level than Jacques Revel, his work as the Parisian director for a large Italian typewriter firm is scarcely more rewarding than are Revel's monotonous translations. He is further plagued by a pious, suspicious wife and an employer wary of the least scandal.

Cécile, his mistress, is a beautiful, cultivated, and sensuous woman, but she clearly owes much of her importance in Delmont's life to the fact that she stands as a symbol of the city in which she resides. Rome magnetically draws Delmont for several reasons. He has only two days earlier passed his forty-fifth birthday and feels his youth quickly vanishing. The warm southern city with its continual spring-time seems to promise a fountain of youth that will wash away the fatigue of his Parisian life (*29*, 34). Like the Crete of Jacques Revel's dreams, Rome is Delmont's land of sensual fulfillment. Henriette, Delmont's wife, wonders why there is a special link between Venus and Rome (*234*, 223). Delmont, on the other hand, knows very well that Venus is Rome's protectress and that she was mother of Aeneas, the city's legendary founder. Venus is also, significantly, the planet which shines on Léon and Cécile's first meeting (*91*, 93). The erotic dimension of Delmont's Roman fixation emerges very clearly in the

Roman divinities of marriage and sex who move through his dreams (*233*, 222) late in the novel.

The ancient Mediterranean civilizations represent a golden age to Butor's heroes because of the full and open acceptance of man's senses and instincts that they represent. Christianity destroyed this primitive innocence by burdening man with its taboos and guilt. Art and religion serve no longer to "deify our instincts, but to terrify them."[1] Passion and sensuality thus become, in Christian societies, a pornographic caricature: the "voluptuous vulgarity"[2] of Paris's "Roman" bar, with its painted nudes and bordello furnishings.

Delmont's life is torn by the conflicting pressures symbolized by the two cities between which he travels. Paris, dominated by his wife and job, represents all that is inauthentic and false in his life. The Roman cafe frequented by his boss Signor Scabelli is significantly the Café de *Paris*. Rome is, in contrast, the center of what he believes to be his truest and deepest loyalties. By committing himself completely and finally to Cécile and Rome, he will heal these divisions and create a "Pax Romana, a world empire organized around a capital city."[3] Delmont plans to announce his new and complete Roman loyalties to Cécile at the Piazza Navona, the center of their Rome (*78*, 82), where Bernini's magnificent fountain of the rivers proclaims Rome's central position in the world (*47*, 50–51). The railroad itinerary which Delmont traces seems to promise a Roman victory over the Parisian portion of his life. He leaves behind the Fontainbleau forest associated with his wife and her fears, passes Alise Sainte-Reine "the scene, according to tradition, of Julius Caesar's victory over the Gauls,"[4] and follows the banks of Lac Bourget, "Lamartine's lake"[5] associated with romantic reverie. And yet somewhere along the line things go wrong and his plans are derailed: he realizes his folly and renounces his Roman project.

Delmont's dreams have been based on a profound misunderstanding of himself and his culture. His beloved Rome is not as he had thought but rather a "prime source of marvels and mysteries."[6] He only dimly perceives the causes of his failure as we leave him, but he has determined to write a book which will examine Rome's mythic power by studying it "in the light of history."[7] Delmont's confusion, like Jacques Revel's amnesia, is the plight of our culture. Butor has shown how some of France's most illustrious writers were pulled between these same poles. Montaigne, nominally a Catholic, regarded ancient Rome as his true home and "sheltered in his heart a philosophical paganism."[8] Racine's plays, generally revered as the work of a great Jansenist Christian, actually contain "a religious structure which was more and more inspired by the paganism of antiquity."[9] Similarly, careful reading of Chateaubriand, the church's greatest nineteenth-century literary defender, reveals the same warfare between the contradictory claims of classicism and Christianity.[10]

And yet the split between the classical and Christian traditions within Western civilization is only part of the problem. If ours were merely a divided culture with two separate and discrete halves, Delmont's solution of choosing one tradition over the other might have been possible. But the situation is more complicated: the two opposing traditions are hopelessly intermingled, preventing a simple option in favor of one or the other. Delmont's voyage of classical escape leads him circuitously back to the Catholic world he tried to flee. During a visit to the Louvre, Delmont sees two large eighteenth-century paintings by Pannini depicting contemporary priests and gentlemen visiting ancient Roman ruins. Delmont discovers in Pannini's portrayal of the contrast between Christian and ancient Rome "the challenge . . . made by the old Roman empire to the existing church."[11] Renaissance Christianity found itself simultaneously dazzled and threatened by the beauty and wisdom achieved by a "pagan" civilization without the aid of divine revelation. The challenge could be met only by assimilating this culture and using it as the "very basis of their language."[12] Already begun in the Middle Ages with Acquinas's "baptism" of Aristotle, the absorption of the classical past became one of the primary goals of the Renaissance. The popes became great collectors of ancient art and learning; Delmont discovers, however, that the Church has not always been a sympathetic or attentive curator of the non-Christian past. In the Vatican Museum he sees an "outstanding masterpiece on which someone has stuck a completely idiotic head, ludicrous arms or feet that rob it of any dignity (and is there nobody within that long-decaying Vatican City to protest against this scandalous confusion, against these fakes?)."[13]

The assimilation, and in many cases the distortion, of the classical past is the theme that runs through the Roman and Parisian art which fills this novel. As in *L'Emploi du temps*, Butor uses artworks as valuable data in his excavation of our culture, but here the works are not imaginary; they are real, famous books, paintings, and buildings. The result is a considerable gain in richness and economy; Butor successfully exploits the historical and cultural resonances of these works to develop his themes.

Delmont has surrounded himself with art that reminds him of Rome. Particularly prized is his copy of Vergil's *Aeneid*, a book he has often carried on his Roman trips. Vergil's epic was an attempt at the moment when Rome had become "the center of the world . . . to justify mythologically this prodigious privilege."[14] Delmont naturally identifies with the epic hero who left behind the wreckage of an earlier life to begin a new one in Italy. On the Monday before his departure, Delmont reads the sixth book of the *Aeneid*. The story of Aeneas's landing in Italy and the glorious predictions of the sibyl and Anchises correspond perfectly with Delmont's dreams of new Italian beginnings. Aeneas also foreshadows Delmont's journey in other ways not anticipated by the Parisian. Delmont will journey underground, literally, as his train enters Mont Cenis tunnel (*135*, 133) and, figuratively, as he follows Aeneas in the Sibyl's cave and Avernus in his dreams (*184, 192*; 179, 186). Delmont dreams of the sibyl who speaks of his father and his future and provides cakes for his journey. The sibyl is, of course, a projection of Delmont's desire to find a new future. Butor reminds us elsewhere that the sibyl functioned as "the center of their universe, the *omphalos*"[15] to whom all Greeks referred their disputes for resolution: she also reflects Delmont's yearning for a center that would reconcile his divided life. But something goes awry in Delmont's mythic dreams: the sibyl denies him the golden bough (*185*, 180) which aided Aeneas, and he finds himself being ferried into Hades, not the Elysian Fields. As the dream progresses, we realize that numerous details are curiously off key. The she-wolf that Delmont encounters reminds us of a similar animal described by Dante in his *Christian* epic of the underworld. The boat which ferries Delmont is without the sails mentioned by Vergil, and Charon the boatman appears in a pose (*189*, 183) which echoes not Vergil but Dante and Michelangelo's *Last Judgment* in the Sistine Chapel.

The latter artist is extremely important in Delmont's dream. Léon and Cécile worship Michelangelo and passionately search out all his Roman work, except for that in the Sistine Chapel. They assiduously avoid the Vatican, the citadel of bourgeois Catholicism, and yet they are "both . . . haunted by those prophets and sibyls, by that absent *Last Judgment*."[16] Despite Delmont's attempts at repression, Michelangelo's magnificent Sistine frescoes force themselves into his consciousness. He describes Henriette as one of the damned who, in the *Last Judgment*, drag others with them (*66*, 68) and names his traveling companions after the prophets and sibyls. His deepest anxieties reveal themselves when he imagines Zechariah, the Old Testament prophet, judging and reproaching him (*171*, 167). Michelangelo's paintings gradually invade Delmont's Vergilian dreams, turning them into a Christian nightmare. The cave through which he walks slowly becomes the marble walls of a chapel (*181*, 177). He

sees the famous painting of the Flood (*226*, 215) and, like Minos in
the Sistine fresco, feels himself constricted by a snake (*226*, 216).
His voyage climaxes not by meeting Anchises, his classical father,
but Christ, Michelangelo's angry judge, who condemns the trembling
Delmont. His true paternity, it turns out, is not classical but Christian.

Delmont is also met by the pope and his cardinals, who reprove
him for his hatred since, according to them, they are the Roman
emperors' true successors (*225*, 215). Their claims make perfect sense
when we consider the fate of Delmont's beloved Vergil. Because
his fourth eclogue was taken as an announcement of Christ's coming,
Vergil "was considered throughout the Middle Ages as the epitome
of that within imperial Rome which made Christian Rome possible,
as the 'pagan prophet.' "[17] He could then serve as the model and
guide for Dante's great Christian epic of sin and redemption. Vergil's and Dante's visions of hell served in turn as sources for Michelangelo's portrayal of the last judgment.

Michelangelo figures crucially in Butor's cultural analysis since
his art reflects the crisis of his age. Irwin Panofsky, the great his-
torian of Renaissance art, describes this crisis as "the cultural
malaise caused by the recent realization of the incompatibility of
medieval Christianity and classicism."[18] The Italian master grounded
his sculpture and painting on a thorough mastery of classical forms
and an understanding of Neoplatonic philosophy. He put these classical elements in the service of Christian subjects such as Moses (*146*,
143), but the wedding was an uneasy one. "Michelangelo's powerful
inhibited figures reflect the disparity between Christian emotion and
the antique ideal, free human will and the will of God: the rational
forms of classic sculpture were not made for the ecstasy of a Christian
mystic, they writhe in the possession of an unfamiliar spirit and be-
tray by brutal distortion, incongruous proportions and discordant
composition the force of the collision of medieval Christianity with
the Renaissance."[19] The Sistine Chapel frescoes are among the greatest
documents of the attempted Christian-classical synthesis. Michelangelo incorporated numerous classical figures (the sibyls, Minos, and the
like) in this grand allegory on man's past and future. But here the
classical is clearly subservient to the Christian: the sibyls are included alongside the Old Testament prophets pointing toward
Christ; Minos is incorporated in a Christian Hell. Christ the Judge
sternly dominates the Chapel; the pervading mood is darkly threat-
ening. "Thus in Michelangelo's last works the dualism between the
Christian and the classical was solved. But it was a solution by way
of surrender."[20]

We discover a similar struggle between Christianity and antiquity in another of Delmont's Roman heroes, Julian the Apostate. Delmont reads Julian's letters on his Roman journeys and clearly identifies with him: Delmont lives in Paris in the service of a Roman (commercial) empire and hopes to emulate the famous emperor by renouncing Christianity and returning to Roman paganism. Delmont fails, but Julian nonetheless proves ironically appropriate to his situation: the Roman apostate's present status curiously resembles that of Vergil described earlier. Delmont visits the Roman baths linked to Julian's years in Paris (*62*, 64). The irony which escapes Delmont but which ought not to escape readers familiar with Delmont's Paris is that these ruins presently lie within precincts which have served as the Parisian residence of the abbots of Cluny and which today are a museum to medieval Christian France. Even Julian has been absorbed, physically if not spiritually, into the Christian world.[21] Delmont's favorite classical landmarks have undergone the same confusing assimilation suffered by Vergil and Julian. The Parisian Panthéon, in whose shadow Delmont lives, is built in the classical style, but was intended as a Catholic church and has several times served that function. Its model, portrayed by Pannini as one of the glories of ancient Rome (*52*, 55), has fared no better: the Roman Pantheon's brass roof was melted down and used to cast Bernini's baldachin in St. Peter's basilica. The final, climactic perversion of imperial Rome was, however, Mussolini's Italy, "intoxicated with her dream of empire,"[22] visited by the honeymooning Delmonts in 1938.

It is not simply the Christian which disturbs Delmont; with Cécile he visits and enjoys Pietro Cavallini's *Last Judgment*. But this painting of the same subject rendered by Michelangelo in the Sistine Chapel is in the Gothic style, uncontaminated by any classical references. What renders the Sistine frescoes and Delmont's dreams so disturbing is the *interpenetration* of the classical and Christian and the *subjugation* of the former by the latter. Thus in Delmont's climactic dream, Christ can condemn Delmont not only in his own name, but also in the name of those many classical figures which surround him in Michelangelo's design (*227*, 217). The would-be Roman sets out following classical models in pursuit of a pagan Golden Age; he blunders, however, and finds himself in a Christian nightmare that leads him back where he began. The confusion is not his alone but ours as well.

Léon Delmont's psyche is a microcosm of his culture: we find in it a mixture of the same contradictory motives and pressures which we have been discussing. At the moment when he believes himself most liberated, Léon is, in fact, acting in a typically bourgeois manner. The train trip is to be his final break with middle-class respectability. His decision to travel third class is motivated, he tells himself, by romantic nostalgia for his first meeting with Cécile in a third-class coach. Actually the choice has been dictated by a much more mundane consideration: he must himself pay for this ticket and fears his wife's detection of the extra expense. The decision to travel third class proves decisive. First, it reminds Delmont of two important disappointments suffered in third class: his honeymoon trip to Rome with Henriette and his abortive attempt to bring Cécile to Paris. It also forces him to take a morning train three hours longer than the more expensive evening train to which he is accustomed. Thus he boards the train poorly rested and unsettled. The crowded third-class coach adds to his discomfort and precipitates his nightmares: his traveling companions become Michelangelo's prophets and sibyls; the serpent of remorse constricting Delmont (*226*, 216) is formed from the zipper of a priest's brief case (*3*, 11) and the compartment's floor grate (*153*, 149).[23] The excessive heat from this same grate contributes to the hellish atmosphere of Delmont's dreams. The longer trip gives Delmont more time to think, dream, and, it turns out, change his mind. As Vivian Mercier points out, "Léon is trapped in a vicious cycle: his bourgeois conditioning is reinforced by the discomfort of the journey, but without this conditioning he would never have bought a third-class ticket in the first place."[24]

Butor's novel is about several different "modifications." A seemingly insignificant rupture of Delmont's usual pattern, the shift from first-class to third-class train accommodations, has important effects. Similarly, the fact that Delmont's trip is made outside the habitual rhythm of his business trips also has its consequences: freed from the commercial concerns that usually distract him from his deeper anxieties, Delmont is forced to confront the truth about the contradictions in his life. Thus, inadvertent physical changes in Delmont's routine help precipitate the larger moral change in the direction of his life. Delmont might well have heeded the warning printed within his compartment (*7*, 15): it is indeed dangerous to lean outside. But there is another modification which is even more crucial in reorienting Delmont's life, the change in the way he sees his past, present, and future.

Delmont's view of time at the novel's outset is symbolized by the railroad timetable which he carries as he boards his train. According to the timetable's linear schema, Paris and Rome exist at opposite ends of a long, black line separated by hundreds of miles of track and hours of travel time. As Delmont proceeds down this line he believes that he is leaving the past, symbolized by Paris at one end, irrevocably behind and moving towards a glorious future, symbolized by Rome, at the other end. The novel recounts events occurring over seventeen years in Delmont's life. As long as these events are kept in their proper linear sequence, separated by many years, Delmont's tranquil optimism is assured. But this one-dimensional model is inadequate: at any point on this straight line he carries countless memories of the past and plans for the future with him. During the course of the present voyage, Delmont recalls or imagines numerous other past or projected trips along the same tracks. These past voyages refuse to rest quietly; they break out of their normal sequence and enter into new relationships with other past events and the present, forcing a new ordering of the future. *La Modification* records a profound shift in Delmont's way of viewing his earlier life and brilliantly demonstrates the dialectical relationship of past and future.

Time in the novel is organized in seven temporal layers: the present, Delmont's projected hopes for the future, and five sequences of memories from the past. Beneath all of these is the even deeper level of repressed anxieties expressed in Delmont's dreams. In planning his novel, Butor used an "algebra" of letters representing these different narrative sequences.[25] Accordingly, I have identified the different temporal levels using the following system:

a: the present, Friday, 15 November 1955, 8:10 A.M. to Saturday, 16 November, 5:45 A.M.
b: the past week, Thursday to Thursday, 7–14 November.
c: Delmont's trip to Paris with Cécile and the return to Rome, November 1954.
d: Delmont's first meeting with Cécile and the ensuing events, August 1953.
e. Delmont's second honeymoon trip to Rome with Henriette, winter 1952.
f: Delmont's first honeymoon trip to Rome, spring 1938.
k: the future, Delmont's plans for his visit to Rome and return. Friday, 15 November, to Tuesday, 19 November.

Delmont's dreams, incorporating details from Vergil, Dante, and Michelangelo and projecting his deepest anxieties, interpenetrate several of these levels. Boldface print will indicate segments containing dreams.

The novel's external organization is neat and carefully balanced: three sections each contain three chapters and roughly the same number of pages. The first section mirrors the initial harmony seen in the overall structure:

I.

1.

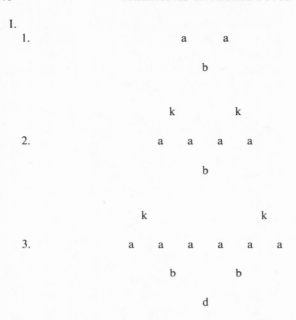

2.

3.

The pattern of narrative sequences in each chapter is symmetrical, the second half of the chapter duplicating in reverse order the pattern of the first half. The first section's symmetries are organized around two glowing moments in Delmont's past, his decision the past week to change his life (b) and his portentous first meeting with Cécile two years earlier (d). Past and future are harmoniously balanced: happy memories and future plans are given equal attention (5:4). But this harmony is superficial; it is possible only because it is temporally shallow and selective. Vast areas of the past remain to be explored.

The fourth chapter probes further into the past and ruptures this symmetrical and harmonious pattern:

II.

4.

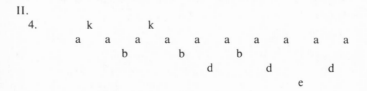

If the procedure instituted in the earlier chapters had been continued, and the pattern established in the first nine segments duplicated in reverse order in the second half of the chapter, the pattern would have been as indicated by the italicized letters in the following schema. The dotted arrows indicate where these segments have been drawn in the new asymmetrical alignment.

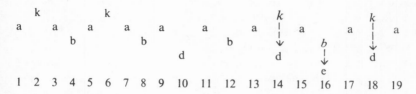

Delmont's problems begin in the eighth segment. Reflecting on the past week (b), he recalls Cécile's mistrusting and reproachful look at the end of their last meeting (*88*, 90), a look disturbingly like the one he confronts daily in his wife's eyes. Fleeing these troubling thoughts, he quite naturally returns in the tenth segment to the happy memories following his first meeting with Cécile (d; *91*, 93). But the unsettling recollections are not disposed of so easily: in section twelve, he recalls his earlier attempt to force Cécile's reproachful look from his mind and remembers dreaming of the accusatory horseman of Fontainebleau (b; *94-95*, 95-97). Once again he attempts to escape back into the early days with Cécile (segment 14, d; *97*, 99). But this deliberate retreat into the past is accomplished at the expense of his plans for the future, which normally ought to have alternated with the past at this point. Delmont breaks the harmonious pattern of the earlier chapters by his efforts to block his dawning awareness. The sequence is drawn further from its anticipated path when the familiar landscape between Mâcon and Bourg (*99*, 100) reminds Delmont of his second honeymoon three years earlier; he is thus drawn into another, deeper layer of the past (segment 16, e). In the fourth chapter, the harmonious symmetry is ruptured, and the relative equilibrium of the past and future is destroyed (the ratio here is 8:2) by the unexpected surfacing of repressed memories.

The disintegration continues in chapter five:

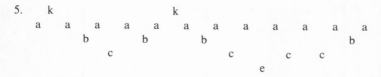

The fond recollections of his earliest days with Cécile (d), which had been the center of chapter three and the sanctuary to which Delmont fled in chapter four, disappear entirely. In their place we have Delmont's painful memories of his abortive attempt to bring Cécile to Paris in 1954 (c). These memories are juxtaposed in this and succeeding chapters with his equally futile attempt to take Henriette to Rome on their second honeymoon (e; *119–28, 149–62*; 119–27, 145–56). Both trips were planned to rejuvenate waning romances, and both failed because of Delmont's inadequacies as a guide: he did not really know either Rome or Paris. The linear chronology which would have kept these events safely separated by two years is destroyed, and these past events are seen in a different perspective. The two past failures cast an ironic light on the present, equally naive attempt to revive a dying affair; they suggest that the present attempt is also doomed and that Delmont must change his plans for the future.

As chapter five ends, Delmont realizes the danger of this descent into the past and attempts to turn his thoughts forward: "stop thinking about that past journey to Paris with Cécile; think only about tomorrow and Rome."[26] Delmont leaves the compartment at the end of each chapter, composes himself, and tries to return to the pattern of alternating the recent past (b) and the future (k) which he had used successfully in section I. But chapter six is even less successful than the preceding chapter: he manages only one sortie into the future before he is drawn back to the fateful Parisian trip with Cecile (c).

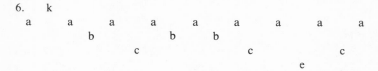

Delmont struggles once again, at the end of chapter six, to escape these memories. He is dimly aware that they are leading him into problems that extend well beyond his own personal case; he fears they may deliver him "not only to the demons in [his] own mind but to all those who haunt [our] race."[27]

In section three these demons surface, forcing their way into the dreams which invade all five temporal levels in chapters seven and eight.

III.

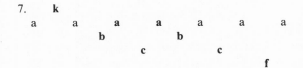

8.   **k**
  a   **a**   **a**   **a**   **a**   **a**   **a**
       b   **b**
              c   **c**
                   f

9.   **k**
  a   a   a   a   a
      b
         c
         f

The ghosts who haunt Delmont's nightmares are born of his repressed personal fears and the confused culture of which he is a product. They overwhelm his last resistance, and near the end of chapter seven, Delmont renounces his hopes for a new life with Cécile. Janus, significantly, makes his first appearance in the dream which interrupts this segment (*198*, 191). This new understanding of the past forces a re-evaluation of the future.

The future segments of chapters one through six have moved steadily forward from Friday through Tuesday. In chapter seven, however, this movement is reversed. The three future segments of chapters seven, eight, and nine recapitulate in reverse order Delmont's projected plans, as the following schema indicates:

I.
2.	*21–23*, 27–29	The continuation of the present through Saturday, 5:45 A.M.
	31–34, 37–39	Saturday 5:45–9:00 A.M.
3.	*42–48*, 48–51	Saturday 9:00 A.M. to sundown
	68–71, 70–72	Sunday 9:00 A.M. to Monday afternoon

II.
4.	*78–80*, 81–83	Monday evening
	83–85, 86–88	Monday night
5.	*107–8*, 107–9	Monday night to Tuesday
	112–14, 112–14	Tuesday
6.	*136–38*, 133–35	Tuesday evening, arrival in Paris

III.
7.	*171–75*, 167–71	Monday evening to Tuesday evening
8.	*207–14*, 200–205	Monday evening
9.	*238–39*, 227–28	Saturday morning to Monday evening

After his discoveries in the past, Delmont's future looks very different. He gradually modifies and then abandons his plans as he retells them from his changing perspective. Compare these two contrasting pairs:

> You'll have said and done all you had to, you'll have settled everything. (Chapter 5; *107*)
> No, everything will not have been said. (Chapter 7; *171*)
>
> You'll take up your post . . . to watch for the opening of her shutters. (Chapter 2; *34*)
> You will not keep watch over Cecile's windows. (Chapter 9; *239*).[28]

One future is disintegrating; a new one is being created. The second segment of the final chapter completes Delmont's revision of his projects for the immediate future, and the first, third, fifth, seventh, and ninth segments all include plans for the novel that will be Delmont's principal task in the future. We see the novel's final and most important modification: Delmont, the self-deceiving typewriter salesman will become a novelist struggling toward self-awareness.

Léon Delmont is, in comparison with Jacques Revel, considerably more sophisticated historically. Avidly interested in ancient Rome, he reads its literature, inspects its monuments, and studies its museums. This knowledge can, however, cause its own kind of ignorance, since total identification and absorption in a single epoch can blind one to what has happened in other periods. Delmont prefers to see his beloved Rome only in the guise it assumed during the Empire, deliberately ignoring what happened to this ancient culture during the Renaissance and counter-Reformation. He exercises a similar selectivity in his personal past, recalling happy moments and attempting to block out his failures. *La Modification*, like *L'Emploi du temps*, recounts the opening of the past; opening the past, as we have seen, also opens the future.

CHAPTER 4

Degrés

La Modification was a prize-winning success at its publication and has since achieved the stature of a classic. Butor's next novel, *Degrés*, had a more mixed reception. Although it was acclaimed by Jean-Paul Sartre, others were perplexed or hostile. After *La Modification*, which despite its many experimental qualities was a novel in the classic French tradition of psychological analysis, many readers must surely have found *Degrés* disconcerting. It has many more characters, none of them sketched with the depth or precision of Léon Delmont; in addition, they are all but drowned in the sea of quotations which inundates Butor's fourth novel. Nevertheless, Butor's basic purposes are the same as in his earlier novels. Pierre Vernier, the Parisian lycée instructor who is the novel's protagonist, shares with Jacques Revel and Léon Delmont the desire to organize and explain the culture in which he lives. He intends to unify the many activities of his lycée students in a single book and, by so doing, to provide a kind of *summa* of our civilization. The book is written for Pierre Eller, Vernier's nephew and pupil. Vernier hopes that by organizing the chaotic mass of learning surrounding Eller he will provide him and his classmates with a "new awareness"[1] of themselves and their culture. He tells his nephew that this literary project will help "you realize what you yourself have been, in other words, where you come from, where you are going—what is the vector of your present."[2]

Revel and Delmont, although they have definite individual characteristics, are intended as representative products of modern Western European culture. In *Degrés* this broad historical portraiture moves even more explicitly to the foreground. The number of characters is substantially increased over the two preceding novels to strengthen the novel's intent to represent an entire society. Even more important (and more disorienting for traditional readers) are the extensive quotations from the authors and manuals studied in the lycée. Secondary education is a vast pastiche of texts, books read by the students and explained by the teachers. We are, Butor believes, what we read: "we are born inside books . . . such that each of us have been *read* before speaking."[3] By listing and quoting the texts by means of which a society shapes its young people, Butor hopes to sketch a psychological profile of that society and chart the "mental space"[4] in which it lives.

Vernier's heroic attempt to organize these materials proves too much, however, and he fails artistically and personally. Exhausted by his task, he falls mortally ill before completing the book, having alienated the nephew the book was meant to help. Vernier realizes that this failure is not his alone but related to larger cultural problems: "these difficulties which now look more and more dizzying on every page, and which are linked to the very contradictions of that society we—students and teachers—constitute, contradictions which I am trying, by means of this text, to present to you so that within yourself at least some of them may be resolved."[5] In this chapter, we will explore those cultural problems which foreordain Vernier's plans to failure. The extraordinary nature of this book, a unique marriage of the novel and a pedagogical compendium, dictates a special methodology. Butor has organized the quoted materials musically, creating themes which reverberate and modulate throughout the novel: "*Degrés* is based on echoes which exist in time . . . it is a study of resonances."[6] We will follow these resonances in the quoted materials and trace the patterns that emerge. These patterns will provide the broad cultural background against which we may view the problems of the individual characters.

Vernier organizes his description of a year's intellectual activity around a special lesson he gives his students on the discovery of America. The lesson is presented on 12 October 1954, Eller's fifteenth birthday and Columbus Day in the United States. Vernier's elaborate preparations indicate that he intends this to be a day of discovery for Eller and his classmates. Vernier and Butor wish to bring the many aspects of contemporary society into relationship with this crucial historical epoch; their intent is to show this period's decisive importance in the formation of our consciousness. Ideas introduced in Vernier's special lecture become recurring themes echoing throughout the academic year and bringing out unexpected, often ironic, undertones in other lessons and readings.

The lesson focuses, Vernier explains several times, on "the discovery and the conquest of America."[7] Discovery and conquest are themes central to the key lecture and thus to the entire novel. Vernier takes as the lesson's starting point texts by Marco Polo and Montaigne. These figures, the former born in 1254 and the latter deceased in 1592, span the Age of Discovery. More important, the Venetian globe-trotter and the French humanist who made his greatest discoveries in the quiet solitude of his tower suggest the two different directions this period's discoveries took: the outward voyages of exploration and the inner examinations that they precipitated.

This period's first and most dramatic achievement was "the sudden multiplication by two of the dimensions of the universe."[8] Marco Polo's travels opened the East, but his writings stimulated another Italian, Christopher Columbus, who extended our boundaries westward as well. The expansionistic energies of the Renaissance were not confined to this globe; explorers trained their eyes on the heavens, discovering new planets studied in geography class. At least as important as the *spatial* doubling was the *temporal* doubling that also occurred during this period. The Renaissance rediscovered Greek and Roman antiquity, an event whose repercussions are felt in the numerous classical (Homer, Vergil, Livy, and so forth) and neoclassical (Racine, Shakespeare's *Julius Caesar*) texts taught in the lycée. Butor uses Keats's "On First Looking into Chapman's Homer" to establish a parallel between these geographical and historical discoveries. At the very moment that Vernier is delivering his key lecture, the English students next door are reading Keats's comparison of his personal discovery of the Greek epic with the Spanish discovery of the Pacific:

> Then felt I like some watcher of the skies
> When a new planet swims into his ken
> Or like stout Cortez when with eagle eyes
> He star'd at the Pacific—and all his men
> Look'd at each other with a wild surmise—
> Silent, upon a peak in Darien[9].

The relationship between the period's great discoveries was more than merely metaphorical. Vernier explains that the success of the geographical discoveries forced Europe to revive its own past: "it was this change in the face of the world that necessitated a change in teaching."[10] The sudden challenge to Europe's geographical centrality in the world caused Europe to seek historical grounds for its claims to world supremacy.

While the Renaissance discoverers were expanding horizons and multiplying knowledge many times over, they were, paradoxically, undermining those structures which in the past had organized such information. The brilliance of the ancients' achievements threatened the medieval authorities and released a corrosive, questioning spirit that soon spread to religion. In his lecture on the Reformation, Vernier explains the "link between the humanist questioning of the scholastic tradition apropos of the literary, scientific or philosophic texts of antiquity and the questioning of the ecclesiastical tradition by Luther apropos of the sacred texts."[11] The new discoveries released divisive energies, and the Renaissance *doubling* became a *splitting*: Europe versus the new worlds, classic versus Christian, Catholic versus Protestant. The continuing struggle of these conflicting authorities surfaces in numerous lessons: Galileo and the papacy (*246, 275*), Montesquieu's ironic religious relativism (*247*, 276), and St. Simon's account of bloody religious persecution (*372, 348, 351*; 303, 386, 389).

The Renaissance simultaneously unleashed a knowledge explosion and interred the medieval world view which had structured the old knowledge around a few universally accepted propositions. Both processes, intellectual expansion and cultural disintegration, have continued to the present day. The result is confusion. Butor explains that in *Degrés* he wanted to "show our culture. . . . We realize the enormity of [the knowledge at our disposal]. So many things, so much confusion. This knowledge that we serve up without correlation to our students, without their being able to understand or assimilate it."[12] The discovery and learning themes modulate ironically into disorder and confusion.

The second theme of Vernier's lecture, conquest, undergoes a similar development, evolving and blending with the themes of exploration, division, and hatred. The subjugation of the American wilderness had powerful consequences for that continent, as we shall see in Butor's American texts, but it dramatically transformed life in the Old World as well. One of the conquerors' principal motives was American gold; the desire for mineral wealth and its importation into Europe contributed to the growth of slavery, capitalism, industrialism, and imperialism. Vernier catalogues the fruits of conquest in his various lectures:

the conquest of America . . . the use of forced labor in the mines, the beginning of the slave trade, the flow of gold into Spain, the development of banks throughout Europe. (*12*)

the growth of capitalism, the development of the railroads and the industrial cities. (*46*)

the transformation of European society after the discovery of America, . . . the rise of the cost of living . . . the remarkable development of the international bankers, Fugger, Medici, the fall of the standard of living in the poor classes. (*159*)

European mercantilism . . . Europe exploits the world. (*205*)[13]

The Renaissance discoveries released economic forces that were to cause new social and racial divisions. Butor's cultural analysis in the earlier novels emphasizes Christianity as the principal source of division; here he introduces an economic factor. Commenting elsewhere on Ezra Pound's contention that usury was the most important source of cultural factionalism, Butor agrees and adds: "There is surely a great deal of truth in this thesis, which is immediately apparent when one gives the word usury its modern equivalent, capitalism."[14] The European's greed for gold blinded him to the New World's natural beauty and its inhabitants' human dignity. Vernier's description of forced labor in the Bolivian mines vividly portrays the brutality, hatred, and smoldering dissension that were this greed's bitter fruits:

> men whose agitation was like the tumult inside a volcano,
> whose despised work, whose forced rage, whose ferment constantly kept in check by police and priests the picture did not show, sent out of the crater a little silver transported with great difficulty, with great losses, with great cruelty, to the harbors and then across the sea to Spain,
> before splitting open this whole new empire, gradually ripening and roasting an enormous secret vengeance (whose smoke would appear only much later), which had doubtless not completed their expansion even today.[15]

Selections from Montaigne's denunciation of European greed, hypocrisy, and cruelty become increasingly important in the novel's final section, echoing and extending the themes seen in the description of the mines (*257, 261, 268, 288*; 287, 291, 299, 321).

The third world has, for the most part, thrown off European political subjugation, but the West's domination survives in other, more subtle ways. The developed world's scientific preeminence shapes the way we view its relationship to the rest of the world. Vernier explains Europe's promulgation of a self-aggrandizing notion of world geography:

> our habitual representation of what is happening in the contemporary world, and of universal history, is constantly distorted by the primacy in our minds of the cylindrical projection, the so-called Mercator projection, used in almost all planispheres, those found in the offices of navigation companies as well as in schools or dictionaries, and which has the peculiarity of considerably enlarging the surfaces of countries in the

> temperate and polar zones to the detriment of those in the equatorial zone,
>
> so that we must often make a considerable effort to appreciate the true relation of masses which exists between nations like France and England on the one hand, for instance, and India or China on the other.[16]

Other measuring systems also insidiously preach European primacy: weight is measured according to a cylinder of irradiated platinum at *Paris* (*31*, 37); time and latitude are calculated from *Greenwich, England* (*32*, 39).

European ethnocentrism shapes the school's entire educational program: the nonwestern world barely appears in Eller's geography and literature lessons; the languages taught are Greek, Latin, Italian, German, and English. This cultural arrogance is particularly apparent in the school's historical studies. Our view of the past defines our attitude toward the present; excluding the rest of the world's contribution to the past justifies excluding these regions from serious consideration today. Butor describes our smug assumption that the *European* historical schema represents *world* history: a "schema which presents itself as sufficient, as capable of explaining everything without bringing in those other peoples, those other civilizations which are bizarre, curious, exotic, and amusing, but which a settled, sober mind, a businessman or politician could not possibly take seriously without appearing ridiculous; such that entities as enormous and prestigious as ancient Egypt or Islam appear in their representation only as appendices, footnotes or rather humorous vignettes."[17]

European cultural myopia and ignorance feed the racial prejudice suffered by Ahmed in *Passage de Milan* and Horace Buck in *L'Emploi du temps*. To these outcasts, Butor adds the mysterious North African glimpsed throughout *Degrés*. This enigmatic figure appears several times, startling Pierre Eller with his harsh, bestial stare (*67*, *339*; 78, 376). Butor has seen the same look in Egyptian faces and understands the anger that it reveals: "the quiet resentment against Europe . . . the envy, the bad feeling, the dolorous and silent need for a reorganization of the world's face."[18] The North African's smoldering resentment has had violent and tragic consequences for France: published in 1960, the novel is set in 1954, the year in which the Algerian War began.

The most serious victims of European ethnocentricity may well be Europeans themselves. The Renaissance discoveries began a geographical shift of power away from Europe that continues today. And yet, Europe, France in particular, chauvinistically resists recognizing this fact. The results, as always when the gap between official dogma and reality becomes too great, are bad faith, anxiety, and more inner contradictions. Vernier deplores "this exclusivity of civilization which it continues to arrogate itself, despite all the proofs which it has unearthed, and which it continues to seek and produce, nourishing this contradiction, this great fissure, this great lie which saps and undermines it."[19]

A picture emerges from the interplay of these themes and texts of a culture that is immense and confused, exploitative and self-deceiving. It is within this cultural context that Vernier, his colleagues, and his students act out their personal dramas. The characters' dilemmas are only individual instances of large cultural problems. "Man," we are told, "is a microcosm."[20] Vernier's personal and artistic failures are the novel's principal tragedy. Granted the immensity of our culture and its divisions, his attempt to organize this enormous material was doomed from the start. The Rabelaisian ideal of total knowledge in the Renaissance was judged to be a "reasonable education," but it proves to be "reasonable for a giant, naturally."[21] Vernier, like most of us, is a man of more modest proportions. Although well-educated and industrious he cannot possibly follow all the lycée's classes and readings. Vernier literally expires under the double burden of attempting to relearn and transcribe the massive body of knowledge; his project is terminated by his physical collapse, "this catastrophe which the book recounts and produces at the same time."[22]

Vernier's problem is not merely to master this learning, but to organize it and the personal stories of his students and colleagues. He believes that this organization will be made possible by a system of family relationships within the school. These relationships will provide him with access to information about his subjects' activities and a structure for organizing this information. But this pattern which Vernier counts on to structure his research reflects the cultural division seen in the lessons. Vernier will treat students and professors in groups of three based on family kinship. The system works reasonably well for the first several triads where the blood ties are fairly close. But in the fifth group, he discovers that to unite M. André du Marnet and M. Tavera, both professors, to their student Hubert Jourdan, he must go back five generations. The relationships grow more tenuous in the sixth group (M. Martin, Jean-Claude Fage, and Henri Fage), where Vernier speculates that "there may have existed, at the end of the fifteenth century, two brothers or two cousins named Fage, who parted at the very moment when Columbus's ships left Cadiz for the first time in search of Cathay, and who never saw each other again, whose descendants never had any connection until the day when two of them converged on Paris."[23]

The relationship between the members of these triads, already very loose in the sixth group because of a separation of a family at the time of the discovery of America, completely breaks down when Vernier tries to relate M. Moret, l'abbé Gollier (the chaplain), and Maurice Tangala. The latter is a black student, "a Negro from the Caribbean, and this whole lesson about America, about the tragedy of America's vengeance, America's riddle, affects him especially."[24] The ties between the priest and Maurice Tangala, whose family was carried from Africa to the New World in slavery "constantly kept in check by police and priests,"[25] are not the usual family relations but "the contrary of links, negative links."[26] The New World's impact on cultural unity manifests itself here in the separation of families and the introduction of an entirely different race into our society. Vernier's personal artistic failure thus reflects the society he would describe; his difficulties in organizing his materials are, he discovers, "linked to the very contradictions of that society we—students and professors—constitute."[27]

The students' personal problems, although less dramatic than Vernier's, also mirror the cultural malaise. Lacking a coherent framework for the mass of information which assails them, they are perplexed and disaffected. Alain Mouron's nightmares, in which Homer, Vergil, Livy, Rabelais, Shakespeare, and Racine merge in a chaotic jumble (333, 370), reflect the confusion suffered by these students. The boys' waking hours are scarcely more pleasant. Positivism reigns supreme in this school named after Hippolyte Taine; the program emphasizes dry memorization of facts with no room for imagination or creativity. The students sense that what is presented as fact is often only subjective interpretation, as in two conflicting portraits of Julius Caesar (25, 30–31), but they dare not question or object.

The youngsters escape school routine by scouting trips into the countryside and by reading fantasy and science fiction, often in the classroom. Butor's children's book Les Petits Miroirs (The Little Mirrors) presents a similar portrait of French student life. The required texts bore Gérard, the bright young hero. He and his classmates find that by inserting a small mirror in their books they can escape into a magic forest where they are instructed by animals not only in the traditional disciplines but in the secrets of airplanes and automobiles as well. Gradually the entire class, teacher included, enters this marvelous world. They love their new studies so much that they regret the summer vacation and the end of classes. Ironically, Gérard's mother, mistakenly attributes her son's new enthusiasm to "the teaching reform."[28] The education described in these two books reveals another form of intellectual imperialism: the adult's imposition of a dry rationalism on the spontaneous, creative mind of a child.

The problems of René Bailly, professor of English, provide another detail in Butor's cultural portrait. They continue the theme of inauthentic romantic escape seen in *La Modification*. Tormented by an unfaithful wife and an unfinished dissertation, Bailly attempts to create another, better life with his mistress (*192*, 217). But, like Léon Delmont, Bailly is guilty of self-deception: he believes himself intellectually liberated, but he sends his children to mass (which he does not attend himself) and worries about the scandal of divorce. Butor contrasts this professor of English ironically with Keats's conquistadores in his failure to break through to a new world (*254*, 283).

Butor also deliberately juxtaposes Bailly's romantic problems with Vernier's, situating key events in both plots on the same day. Bailly's wife leaves to join her lover in Orléans while Vernier and Micheline Pavin are meeting for the first time (*263*, 293). The English professor discovers his wife's infidelity and has a major fight with her on the night that Vernier prepares his key lesson (*230–3*, 259–61). Bailly's bad faith contrasts with Vernier's attempt to confront and understand his experience through writing. Like Delmont, Vernier was tempted to center his life on a woman associated in his mind with the classical past. During the preceding summer, he traveled to Delphi and Delos where he first meets Micheline, who remains associated in his mind with these sites (*120*, 136). Vernier soon finds that he must choose between literature and marriage (*142*, 162); although he remains close to Micheline, Vernier chooses literature. Unlike Bailly who uses sex as an escape, Vernier uses it as a creative spur; he asks Micheline to order him to continue his work, and she does so (*152*, 172).

The contrast with Bailly prevents us from seeing Vernier exclusively as a failure. Despite his difficulties, he is clearly headed in the proper direction. As Vernier lies ill, Henri Jouret describes his book as "a ruin," but he also recognizes in it the "fragment of a consciousness and of a future music."[29] Butor explains that Vernier's death is not in vain: "There had to be this sacrifice within the novel. Insofar as he accepts . . . being this victim, he succeeds. Insofar as he realizes that 'that future music' is denied him but that his death will render it possible for others, he is entirely forgiven."[30] Vernier's "failure" succeeds by revealing our cultural shortcomings and demonstrating the arduous analysis that will be necessary if these problems are to be understood and resolved. Vernier will not see these solutions, but his work has moved us nearer to their realization.

Montaigne and Marco Polo, the cornerstones of Vernier's lecture, become his models in a way he could not have anticipated. Montaigne, despairing of success in his own time, hoped for the collaboration of "a future friend who will fill the place ready for him."[31] Similarly, Voltaire, quoted on the novel's penultimate page, reminds us that Marco Polo's narrative lay long ignored, requiring a Columbus to exploit its significance. Vernier's work, like Jacques Revel's, is and must be incomplete. In its incompleteness, it invites us to continue the construction of this "tower from which one was supposed to be able to see America."[32]

Degrés differs significantly from Butor's earlier novels. *La Modification* succeeded brilliantly in presenting a psychologically complex and interesting protagonist, but this success was, in a sense, a failure if readers saw only this individual and not the larger cultural problems he was meant to represent. The characters of *Degrés* share our attention with the literary, scientific, and popular texts which here replace the earlier novels' artworks as Butor's principal cultural data. The primary repository of our cultural identity has, since Gutenberg, been the printed page and the library. Butor realizes that if he wishes to change our understanding of our culture he must change our understanding of the texts upon which it is based.

Embedded in official handbooks and bibliographies, important texts lose their power in our lives. Butor attacks this fossilized literary order: he rips quotations from their traditional contexts, juxtaposes them with other texts and thrusts them into relationship with the lives they are meant to illuminate. Montaigne's denunciation of the European conqueror's greed and hypocrisy is given to us gradually, forcing us to attend to the developing description of cruelty and see its relation to other instances of exploitation. Rabelais's four-hundred-year-old call for educational reform, a quasi-sacred text for French "humanist" educators, echoes hollowly through the dreary lives of the Lycée Taine's teachers and students.

The quotation was, of course, a favorite Renaissance device, as both Rabelais's and Montagne's works attest; and Butor, in a sense, imitates his masters. But merely to mention these writers suggests the contrast between their age and ours. The Renaissance author's art of quoting, as Hans Mayer explains, "reveals his participation in the riches of the Western cultural tradition. He can refer to it and draw upon it with the justified confidence that his audience does not stand fully outside this tradition. The continuity of the cultural tradition guarantees a certain community of general cultural horizons."[33] Butor's quotations, however, function very differently. Pierre Vernier does not dominate his materials; on the contrary, he is dominated and finally destroyed by them. Fragments of Homer, Vergil, and Dante are broken and jumbled with modern physics, geography, and chemistry. The result is a feeling of profound cultural disarray.

Degrés also differs in its narrative point of view. Butor regretted that the omniscient perspective of *Passage de Milan* distanced the reader from the problems described. The first person narration in *L'Emploi du temps* joins the reader directly to the protagonist's fevered mind as he struggles toward awareness. *La Modification*'s accusatory second person narration simultaneously addresses Léon Delmont and the reader. *Degrés* continues this search for a perspective that will transform the reader's passivity into active involvement. Pierre Vernier intends his book as a guide for his young nephew, and, in the first section, he often addresses his young pupil-reader directly in the second-person "tu" form. The second section, seeking to view problems from the pupil's perspective, uses Pierre Eller's first-person account. Vernier wishes to involve his young student directly, but as we soon discover, this involvement is a sham. Eller has not spoken in the second section; rather Vernier has simply continued the narrative in his nephew's name. Eller, who has never been allowed to do more than spy and report on his friends, becomes disillusioned and breaks with his uncle. This break upsets Vernier emotionally, cuts off his information, and contributes significantly to his failure and physical collapse.

The death of this pedagogue-author-narrator is enormously significant not only in this novel but in Butor's work as a whole. It reveals, as we have seen, the impossibility of a single modern figure embracing the whole of his culture in the way that Rabelais was able to do in the Renaissance. More important in the present context, it reveals Butor's disenchantment with the notion of the author who, through a narrator-surrogate within his work, delivers us a neat lesson. "The author," Butor tells us, "is in the classroom with his readers. The text does not pass from the author-professor to the reader-listener-pupil; it is born from the students' dialogue among themselves. The author is the agent who makes possible the transforming stabilization of a narrative which is already present."[34] Butor dramatizes the tensions within our civilization by contrasting key texts and events. By leaving these tensions unresolved he encourages our own active consideration of these problems.

It is significant that Vernier's supposedly multiple point of view becomes truly multiple only after his death when Henri Jouret takes up the narrative. The novel begins with the pedagogue confidently ascending his podium and ends with his death and the words "who speaks?" If the novel has been successful, we have heard the voices speaking within our culture and are now prepared to make our own contribution to the discussion. The unique structure of *Degrés* is of a piece with its themes, for by means of it Butor seeks to rekindle the Renaissance capacities to discover and question. Butor's subsequent works will explore even more aggressively the "open narrative." *Degrés*, Butor's last novel, anticipates, both thematically and structurally, the experimental American texts that follow it.

CHAPTER 5

Description de San Marco
and
Portrait d'artiste en jeune singe

With *Degrés*, his last novel, Butor completed the general outlines of his survey of Europe's cultural roots: Egypt, Greece, Rome, and the Renaissance. And yet there remained a number of significant lacunae which he would attempt to fill with two additional European texts: *Description de San Marco* (1963) and *Portrait d'artiste en jeune singe* (1967). Although these books were published during the same period as his first two American texts, they belong thematically in the European world of the novels, and we will first discuss them before crossing the Atlantic.

During the year he spent teaching in Salonika, a city removed from the centers of classic Hellenism, Butor became aware of another Greece, that of Byzantium, which has also contributed significantly to our culture: "Salonika, halfway between Athens and Constantinople, . . . is the perfect place to experience the proof, so often ignored, that between the dazzling Hellenic civilization and our time there is not only that path which passes through Rome and the Italian Renaissance, but also, intersecting it more than we might imagine, one blazed by the monuments of the Eastern Empire and Church."[1] Pierre Vernier describes the glories of Constantinople in an attempt to make his history students feel the "poignant Byzantine splendor,"[2] but generally speaking, Byzantium's contribution is poorly understood and rarely acknowledged. Venice, mistress of the Adriatic and Western Europe's gateway to Constantinople, was the principal beneficiary of the Crusaders' sack of that city. St. Mark's, Venice's great basilica "where East and West meet,"[3] is an excellent place to study Western

Christianity's encounter with Byzantium. This church is the subject of Butor's *Description*.

At first glance, *Description de San Marco* bears a striking resemblance to *Mobile* (1962), the American text that it followed by a year: the same juxtaposition of different texts, margins, and types. On a deeper level, however, the structure more closely resembles that of *L'Emploi du temps*. Butor's second novel consists of five chapters, the first and last of which are entitled "L'Entrée" and "L'Adieu." They describe Jacques Revel's gradual penetration of Bleston's mysteries, an exploit patterned on Theseus' tracing of the Cretan labyrinth. *Description* also consists of five chapters, "La Façade," "Le Vestibule," "L'Intérieur," and so forth, which chart Butor's progress into the heart of this basilica aided by an Ariadne's thread of texts and images inscribed on its walls and ceiling. This architectural masterpiece provides lessons similar to those which Jacques Revel reads in Bleston's monuments. Like the Old Cathedral, San Marco recounts the relations between several peoples and several epochs. The façade provides the keynote. The history of its famous bronze horses summarizes the successive claims to supremacy of a whole series of cultures: this group of Greek statues was "doubtlessly selected by Nero to crown his triumphal arch, transported by Constantine to his new Rome where it crowned the hippodrome, and finally carried off b' Napoleon for the triumphal arch of the Carousel, where it remaine until the Congress of Vienna ordered its return."[4]

The most important claims are, of course, those of the Serene Republic herself. San Marco's façade conspicuously displays the spoils of Constantinople and other Eastern civilizations (20) and boldly asserts Venice's rights as their successor. But military and cultural supremacy are two different matters. The very trophies which proved Venice's political domination also advertise the prodigious artistic achievements of her supposedly subjugated predecessors. The Venetian response was not unlike the one recorded earlier by Pannini when he contrasted classic and Christian Rome: "it was impossible that visitors be given the impression that all St. Mark's splendor was derived from the great imperial city fountainhead. All this must be enclosed in a new fabric."[5] As in Christian Rome, the younger culture strove to assimilate and surpass its predecessor. The display case would outshine its trophies: "the basilica is so powerful that she absorbs into her wall the very body of her enemies."[6] The basilica's Byzantine architectural style affirms the continuity between Venice and Constantinople; at the same time, it manipulates and violates these forms in a manner that asserts the church's independence from the source of its inspiration. The thirteenth-century Gothic rose window proclaims precisely this fact: it is a "flagrant and deliberate violation of the Byzantine tradition, underlining everything that was not Byzantine in the area's mosaics."[7]

The basilica's interior provides further revelations. As we penetrate the vestibule, we discover that this building is not merely an architecture of bricks and mortar but "an architecture of images . . . an architecture of texts":[8] the visual and literary decorations are disposed in such a way as to tell a particular story. The sources for these artistic and textual decorations are, of course, the Bible and Christian tradition, but these basic elements are organized and shaped to make local and secular assertions as well. Butor reminds us of what Revel learned earlier in Bleston, that religious traditions are always molded by local cultural pressures; "the Bible of St. Mark's will give us a Venetian adaptation of Catholicism often quite different from the Roman tradition."[9]

Certain elements of Biblical history are given special emphasis because of their particular relevance to Venice. The Venetian interpretation of Genesis asserts the city's rights to international hegemony: " '. . . Then God shaped man from the clay of the earth,' a version particularly interesting for Venice, linking man's birth to the separation of the clay and the waters, to the constitution of the Venetian archipelago. The lagoon reproduced humanity's origins, the inhabitants acquired by this very fact an authority, a right over others."[10] The portraits of Babel and Pentecost make similar claims for Venice's primacy among nations (45–46, 88). The artists exploit Venice's situation as a city surrounded by water to draw an analogy between Noah's ark and the basilica (40), a spiritual ark protecting Venetians from the depths, literal and metaphorical.

The church vestibule through which one enters displays scenes from the Old Testament; the baptistry and chapels through which one exits are devoted primarily to the New Testament and the early Christian era. These areas exist in time: in them one is concerned with Christian *history*. The central section of the church and of Butor's book is organized around the climactic moment in the Christian schema which exists outside time. Large mosaic panels portray the Old Testament prophets and their predictions of the Savior to come: Ezekiel, Solomon, David, Isaiah (67, 73–74, 82–83). They point toward the Pantocrator enshrined above the altar. The Christian view of history is essentially eschatological, seeing all human and divine events moving toward the creation of the New Jerusalem after the last judgment. Bleston's Old Cathedral windows were originally intended to climax in a portrait of this Celestial City. San Marco's architects share this view and illustrate it in their design. They add, however, secular elements of their own. Butor describes the manner in which Venice conceives the culminating event at the end of history: "above the large pulpit, the conclusion of all this, the universal Judgment, paradise at the top and, by the large bay, what ought to be the Heavenly Jerusalem, Venice, the sky of Venice."[11] Venice and the City of God merge in this unique eschatological vision.

Butor notes elsewhere the manner in which Albrecht Dürer and the architect of Paris's St. Eustache[12] model their heavenly cities on real, contemporary models, implying the continuity of the City of Man and the City of God. Nowhere, however, is the interpenetration of the secular and the sacred asserted with greater force than above San Marco's altar, where the Venetian architects, deliberately violating Byzantine conventions, pierce the ceiling and replace New Jerusalem with Venice's blue sky. To appreciate the profound implications of this architectural gesture, we have only to contrast San Marco with others of Butor's churches. The soot-darkened interior of Bleston's Old Cathedral, bereft of its culminating City of God window, leaves its confused worshippers with no vision of the future. The Sistine Chapel is an even more dramatic contrast. This windowless interior, immured within the Vatican, prophesies a terrifying future in which the wrathful judge waits to condemn all that is of the flesh.

Butor delights in Venice's sensual richness. He first came to the city just after his two years in Manchester. His reaction was utter stupefaction; San Marco's famous façade glimmered like a jewelled rainbow[13] before his delighted eyes. Little wonder that Butor returned to Venice on his honeymoon. Venice's status as the European honeymoon capital is reflected in the chorus of tourist voices which punctuate the text: the background noises abound in references to the seductive hair, lips, and dress of the city's female visitors. Voices whisper caressing words of love—"Je t'aime" (93), "Love. . . . T'aime" (94), "Je t'aime" (95), "Tu es belle—Bella donna" (97)—suffusing the text with a romantic, faintly erotic glow. Venice has always been the most oriental of Western European cities. Through the Adriatic it opens into the Mediterranean and the ancient Greek and Egyptian cradles of civilization. More than any other Western city, Venice has embraced the pagan, sensual freedom which, for Butor, has always held the best hope for realizing the New Jerusalem on earth.

Portrait d'artiste en jeune singe (1967) followed *Description de San Marco* by four years. The book recounts Butor's trip to Bavaria in the summer of 1950, but its flyleaf informs us that this excursion was "also a voyage in time: the eighteenth century was barely drawing to a close in several isolated areas of this region, the twilight of the Holy Roman Empire."[14] Butor told Jacqueline Piatier that in *Portrait* he attempted "to do a composition in the eighteenth-century German style with all its medieval remnants, and thus to express our profound relation with the Middle Ages."[15] *Portrait* thus fills an important geographical and historical gap in Butor's cultural explorations—central Europe during the years of the Holy Roman Empire, the Middle Ages through the eighteenth century.

Butor has long been fascinated by this epoch and, in particular, by the alchemical studies it nurtured. Butor values alchemy highly and disagrees with the common opinion which regards it as a clumsy and superstitious paleo-chemistry. He blames this rejection on a failure to recognize alchemy's true nature; its aims are not primarily scientific but philosophical, religious, and poetic. While alchemists did seek to transmute base metals into gold, these activities were a symbolic code for describing a more important ascetic transformation of the adept to a higher level of consciousness. The different elements and processes in the physical experiments all had numerous symbolic associations in this spiritual process. The "scientific" books left by these experimenters are in reality works of great poetic imagination. The goal of the alchemical quest was a single work, a "super book"[16] which would unite and explain all reality, physical and spiritual, within a single coherent system.

This quest for an all-encompassing book must surely have struck a responsive chord in Butor; his protagonists—Revel, Delmont, and Vernier—all seek to organize their lives through literature. Butor saw in alchemy an effort to reconcile or transcend the polarity that plagued such characters: "the Christian dichotomy, matter and spirit, which leads to Cartesian dualism."[17] The alchemical synthesis also includes Butor's temporal dialectics of past and future. The alchemist is a "mental archeologist"[18] who descends into the past to retrieve a lost art; at the same time, he hopes through this art to transmute base metal into the gold from which the New Jerusalem will be built.[19] Alchemy thus stands as a symbol of Butor's own artistic activity, and this account of his education as an alchemical "monkey" is also the story of his beginnings as an artist.

We learn in the *Portrait*'s first section of young Butor's avid readings in alchemical books preserved within his family and of his conversation with a Hungarian doctor and alchemical scholar. The middle section tells of Butor's trip to Germany, arranged by his Hungarian friend, to serve as the conversational companion of a German count. The count's ancient castle, "a bubble of past time,"[20] contains a rich alchemical library which enables Butor to pursue his studies and steep himself in the medieval atmosphere. The narrative ends with Butor's departure for Egypt, where he will begin his first novel.

But Butor discovers more than alchemy in the old Empire. This medieval world was in communication not only with Alexandrian Egypt but also with Hungary—"that patch of Asia"[21] which evokes Nosferatu, vampires, and Attila the Hun. The middle section's eight daylight chapters describing Butor's German explorations are interspersed with seven chapters recounting fantastic dreams of Hungary and vampires. Daytime occurrences and readings reappear, strangely transformed in these nightmares. As the young artist explores the castle's library, he trips an alarm which he initially mistakes for the air raid sirens of the recent war (104). Startled by this event, he discovers menacing forces lying dormant within this forgotten castle: "I knew that the cell's silence was like a frail bridge built over a howling gulf."[22]

Butor's dreams clarify the nature of his fears. The night before he trips the alarm, he imagines himself descending into an underground chamber where he meets a beautiful young student. Despite the young lady's warning, Butor deliberately destroys a switch like the one he will accidentally activate the next day. The next night he finds that the sounding of this alarm has summoned into his dreams a vampire dressed as a fantastic German officer (113–14). Butor's source for the visions which punctuate *Portrait* is the *Thousand and One Nights'* "Second Calendar's Tale." The corresponding figure in the original tale is simply a genie; Butor changes him into a Nazi vampire to underscore the special character of the dark forces hiding in the German night. Similarly, the Arab bandits who rob the young scribe in the "Second Calendar's Tale" become in Butor's dreams seven tanks and a group of pillaging soldiers (64).

These dreams echo other references to World War II in *Portrait*. Butor remembers the German trucks in Paris (38, 41) and two earlier trips to Germany, one for military training during the war and the other for "denazification" after the war (46). During his current visit to Bavaria, he sees the war's effects everywhere: his host has lost a brother in Russia (59), and he finds a synagogue that survived only because it had been turned into a barn (168). He visits Munich's ruined Pinakotek museum and the Nazi Haus der Kunst (203). American bombers periodically drone overhead (105, 207). Butor deliberately inserts these contemporary references into this "medieval" adventure to make it something more than Romantic nostalgia. The monsters whose roots are here are real; they wear stormtroopers' boots as well as vampire wings.

Butor discovers a mysterious world in which brilliant flights of philosophical and poetic imagination exist side by side with strange, barbaric practices. The castle contains a torture chamber as well as a library. Even more disconcerting for the young adept, the realms of alchemy and vampires strangely interpenetrate. The underground chamber in which he meets the vampire is described as "the philosopher's abode,"[23] echoing the title of Fulcanelli's famous alchemical treatise (56). The young girl he meets there is, in fact, Fulcanelli's daughter, who promises to be his lover but warns him that she is also the vampire's mistress.

Butor learns that one does not traffic easily with these mysterious forces. During an alchemical revery he imagines uttering the magic "Marantha" (154) and soaring marvelously into the heavens. Ironically, the switch that he breaks bears this same word (91), but it summons the vampire, who carries him off on a flight very different from the one anticipated. Alchemy promises to open the adept's eyes and enable him to see the light that is hidden to others (34); in fact, Butor, both in his dreams and in reality, suffers a painful injury that nearly closes one of his eyes. The first four daylight chapters contain numerous excerpts from Butor's alchemical readings; the second four include passages from a catalogue of people burned, beheaded, or tortured in a nearby castle. The names of the unfortunate victims become progressively more insistent in the final chapters, contesting the alchemical readings (206–14) and infiltrating Butor's dreams. Frightened, his eye aching, and an American bomber droning in his ears, Butor invokes benevolent artistic and philosophical forces to protect him against the specters raised by the recital of tortures:

> Oh beauty, protect me, beauty! . . .
> Oh clarity, protect me! . . .
> against the horror which gnaws protect me! . . .
> against these growlings, against these gruntings,
> against these crackings, against these
> roarings, against these sneerings.[24]

Alchemy and bestial tortures coexist in the medieval darkness. They are, in fact, two aspects of the dark German genius, so different from orderly French rationalism. The same Teutonic imagination that produced incredible poetic flights has shown itself capable of the most irrational cruelty. The young Butor notices early on that one of his alchemical texts appears to be printed on human skin (28). These texts tell us in fact that alchemy depends on the interaction of opposed forces (134, 188). As Léon Delmont learned in *La Modification*, historical selectivity is impossible. One must confront honestly everything one finds in an epoch or a place. This is particularly important for Butor since this is his past: he has Hungarian blood flowing in his veins, and there are even family stories of an ancestor who rode with Attila the Hun.

Both *Portrait* and *Degrés* are the stories of an education, and both combine narrative with extensive quotations from the works studied. But the types of education and the texts studied are utterly different in these two books. The educational program of *Degrés* emphasizes French literature, the Renaissance, and science. The Middle Ages, except for a passing reference to Dante, scarcely appear. Gargantua's letter to Pantagruel, a key text in these lessons, is a joyous cry of relief that the medieval night has finally ended. *Portrait*, on the other hand, is a kind of "contre-*Degrés*"; the emphasis is on Germany and Hungary, the Middle Ages, and alchemy. In contrast to the Lycée Taine's sterile positivism, *Portrait* proposes a program of richly imaginative works. Butor's extracurricular reading list includes the alchemists and a whole tradition of literary fantasy—Jules Verne, H. P. Lovecraft, and science fiction—usually excluded from serious academic programs. Pierre Vernier's pupils, who surreptitiously retreat into fantasy and science fiction, hunger for precisely such a corrective to the traditional curriculum.

Degrés describes the destruction of an artist; *Portrait* describes the making of an artist. Butor is fully aware of what demons as well as what beauties lie within the irrational and the unconscious, but, like the surrealists, he knows that the true artist must tap these forces and include them if he is to provide a genuine synthesis of our culture. The descent into this darkness has in Butor's case been efficacious. The third section, the flight to Egypt, is blank, but we know its outcome. The name on the cover, Michel Butor, is the name of its protagonist: the alchemical transubstantiation has taken place, and the young adept is now an artist of international reputation.

Unlike *Degrés*, where all is apparent disorder, *Portrait*'s narrative is coherently organized; and this organization flows directly from its alchemical subject matter. Jennifer Waelti-Walters and Thomas O'Donnell have shown Butor's elaborate use of alchemical ideas to structure his narrative.[25] The book is divided into three sections; the first contains five chapters, the second has fifteen chapters, including seven which occur at night. The book covers eight days (Monday through Monday) and seven nights from seven weeks. The numbers three, five, seven, and fifteen all have important alchemical significance. Other instances of numerological, mineralogical, and color symbolism from alchemy occur throughout *Portrait*. Daytime and dream, autobiography and symbolism, realism and surrealist fantasy combine in this work. The book attempts to be that which it describes, an introduction and an enticement to a richly imaginative medieval world.

CHAPTER 6

Mobile

Michel Butor's favorite historical figure is Christopher Columbus;[1] it was inevitable that Butor should follow this famous explorer to the New World in search of his own discoveries. The momentum of Butor's work seems to have been at least as important as the invitation of the Bryn Mawr French department in drawing him to the United States for the first time in 1959. The cultural backgrounds of his novels move steadily westward and forward: Egypt, Greece, Rome, Renaissance France, and Spain. *Degrés*, the "tower from which one was supposed to see America,"[2] already points beyond the Atlantic. Once on the new continent, Butor found his curiosity drawing him into an intensive study of its every area. This voracious interest is still unsated after four lengthy stays (1959–60, 1962–63, 1969–70, 1973–74), and Butor now plans to spend every fourth or fifth year teaching in the States. This American fascination significantly influenced Butor's writings; he has in the last decade and a half produced three long narratives (*Mobile*, *6.810.000 litres d'eau par seconde*, and *Où, Le génie du lieu, 2*) and numerous shorter pieces on the United States.

This fascination is easily understood, for America is especially valuable to a writer seeking to grasp both the past and the future. American history, in its earliest stages, was largely the story of the transplanting of European institutions, values, and vices in the new soil. The European traveling in the United States thus finds himself making "a voyage within his own history, . . . within his own contradictions."[3] But a trip across modern America, ahead of Europe in so many material ways, is also "a kind of journey into the future, not only because you find today in the States a few gadgets that will come to France one or two years from now, but because certain problems are already apparent here whereas there they are still hidden."[4]

Butor's familiar archeological metaphor recurs in his description of *Mobile*: "I explored archeologically this very lively country."[5] The purpose here is to understand the American *mobiles*, the motives and drives which cause Americans to act as they do. These answers can be found only by digging into the American and European past. We will meet, as we explore this new continent, many of the ghosts that haunt the dreams of Revel, Delmont, and Vernier. The European newcomers arrived in America "with their European problems and contradictions, which found a space in which these contradictions, in a certain sense, flourished. . . . The problem of the United States is the problem of what happens to European civilization when it arrives in a landscape that permits it to develop on a larger scale."[6] Butor emphasizes the links between Europe and America by referring to America's white inhabitants as "Europeans."

Mobile differs strikingly from Butor's earlier works. There are no characters or plot in the traditional sense; instead we find fifty chapters, each devoted to one of the fifty states, which provide an abundance of descriptive and interpretive material about this country. The chapters are linked by the repetition of town names found in several states as well as by the longer continuing texts. *Mobile*'s verbal materials can be divided into several categories. There is first of all the material in roman type which serves as the text's skeletal framework. A welcoming sign introducing different states and town names appears in roman capitals. County names, the time, road signs, and brief physical descriptions of individual states are given in lower-case roman.[7]

Around this scaffolding Butor has grouped a wide variety of materials in italic. Short italicized phrases and words are sprinkled across the page, presenting natural and cultural features characteristic of a particular area. The listing of American birds, plant and marine life, and catalogues of foreign-language radio broadcasts, newspapers, and foreign cuisines suggest America's extraordinary physical and ethnic diversity. Longer italicized texts—commentaries, catalogues, and selections from the writings of famous Americans—continue over several chapters and serve a different function. In contrast to the shorter elements, which are local in their emphasis, the longer "national" texts are meant to suggest what is unique and distinctive in American culture as a whole. The opposition of the brief, fragmented italic elements and the longer italicized texts may be viewed as the distinction between rich local diversity and national cultural identity.

Despite its unorthodox form, *Mobile* is a travel narrative—the account, as the back cover informs us, of a voyage "across a continent, across the centuries."[8] We are the travelers, and Butor is our guide. He has carefully structured this voyage-text, choosing his materials for their ability to reveal significant aspects of American culture and for their capacity to interact with other texts. The book's chapters and unique typography permit us to enter and leave the text where and when we choose. The title suggests an analogy with Alexander Calder's mobile sculptures, which may be seen from many different perspectives. And yet our freedom in exploring this text is conditioned by the nature of its linguistic medium. Sentences move in a definite direction: from left to right and from top to bottom. Once in the text, we are caught by its momentum, which pulls us forward toward certain key encounters.

Mobile, like Butor's other narratives, is organized around the temporal unities and the rhythms of light and darkness that they encompass. Its fifty chapters treat the fifty states in alphabetical order over forty-eight hours (South Dakota and Delaware share the same hour as do Idaho and Illinois). The chapters thus are grouped into five sections distinguished by this alternation of night and day:

1. Alabama, Alaska, Arizona,   3:00 A.M. EST–4:00 A.M. PST
   Arkansas, California

2. North Carolina, South Carolina,   8:00 A.M. EST–7:00 P.M. CST
   Colorado, Connecticut, North
   Dakota, South Dakota, Delaware,
   Florida, Georgia, Hawaii, Idaho,
   Illinois, Indiana, Iowa, Kansas

3. Kentucky, Louisiana, Maine,   8:00 P.M. CST–6:00 A.M. MST
   Maryland, Massachusetts, Michigan,
   Minnesota, Mississippi, Missouri,
   Montana, Nebraska, Nevada

4. New Hampshire, New Jersey,   9:00 A.M. EST–7:00 P.M. MST
   New Mexico, New York, Ohio,
   Oklahoma, Oregon, Pennsylvania,
   Rhode Island, Tennessee, Texas, Utah

5. Vermont, Virginia, West Virginia, 9:00 P.M. EST–12:00 P.M. MST
   Washington, Wisconsin, Wyoming   (2:00 A.M. EST)

The chapters are almost evenly divided between the hours of daylight and the hours of darkness: twenty-four states are in the former category and twenty-six in the latter. The book's first, third, and final sections occur at night, while the second and fourth sections are in the day. There is considerable similarity in the material contained in these alternating sections, but there are several important differences. The introductory road signs to each state disappear, and the short, descriptive italic fragments become less numerous. The night darkness dims our sight, and we lose the physical clues to our precise geographical location. The longer italic texts are less frequent at night and, in contrast with the historical and sociological texts presented in daylight, consist primarily of the dreams of anonymous Americans. (One of the few historical texts presented at night is the nightmarish account of the Salem witch trials.) The day texts are psychologically revealing indirectly, but the night dreams emanate directly from the deepest and most repressed levels of the American consciousness. The day-night distinction is, in this respect, one between relative depths in the American psyche.

The reader may enter the text at any point and read in any direction, but, if he reads the entire text, he must inevitably submit himself to these fundamental day-night rhythms. The reader is now the protagonist and, like Jacques Revel and Léon Delmont, must undergo the initiatory ordeal of the descent into darkness. We discover at the center of this descent, which is near the center of the book, an ironic parody of the *omphalos*, the "center" of the American world. Maryland, the twenty-fourth of the fifty chapters, is set at midnight, the end of the first day. Here we make a pilgrimage to Washington D.C., America's religious center, and penetrate the mysteries of its unique cult:

> The most important religious practice of the American Europeans is the pilgrimage to the sacred city of Washington, where the principal temples and the essential government organizations are located. . . . The quasi-rectangular territory of this city (it is well known what fundamental value the American Europeans have attached to the right angle) is an enclave within the state of Maryland, but forms no part of it. It is a space apart.[9]

Washington D.C. is, of course, America's political center, and its monuments memorialize real historical figures, but Butor's analysis insists that this place has a deeper religious function as well. He maintains that Washington, Jefferson, and Lincoln enjoy quasi-divine status (*126*, 132) and notes the awesome respect with which the Constitution and other "sacred" papers are regarded (*129*, 135). As in primitive religion, ancestor worship and the veneration of cult objects guarantee the cohesion of the nation: "*The religion of Washington is the only one to be practiced by all the American Europeans.*"[10] He also directs our attention to the dazzling whiteness of these monuments and the obvious racial implications of this color for the European American majority (*128*, 134).

But Washington D.C. is only an apparent center, the focus of one level of America's loyalties. This description of American religion occurs in a night section where it is contradicted by dreams that reveal

very different and conflicting tensions in the American psyche. To
properly understand the significance of these dreams and their disrup-
tive power, we must look at Butor's analysis of the American immigrant's failure to meet and exploit the extraordinary possibilities offered
by the new world. The American continent offered Europe an opportunity to heal its divided soul. The Ralon brothers, Jacques Revel, and
Léon Delmont all suffer acute cultural schizophrenia: how to choose
between the canonical Christian virtues and the enormously seductive,
ancient "pagan" ideals. The options were two entirely different and
opposed approaches to life: Judeo-Christian restraint versus Mediterranean sensuality. Chateaubriand, writing early in the nineteenth century, defined the cancer gnawing Europe's vitals as "the war between
two systems of contradictory values: the 'Christian' and the 'classical.' "[11] The war's greatest casualty was the integrity of the human
personality: the Christian-pagan opposition translated within Western
man's torn psyche into the opposition of spirit versus body. We have
seen the devastating consequences. Rose Bailly's tightly buttoned
sweater and the pornographic nudes of Paris's "Roman" bar are
products of the same sexual repression and guilt. The body is ignored—
or enjoyed only furtively and guiltily.

The New World provided a chance to solve this cultural crisis, not
by eliminating one of the warring traditions, but by introducing a third
force. The wild new landscape invited the European to imitate another
cultural model, the Indian. The red man fascinated the European imagination because of his obvious pride in and enjoyment of his body: "The
dream of becoming Savage is above all the hope for an erotic liberation
and that is why the decisive characteristic of the state of nature is
nudity."[12] The Indian's extraordinary acceptance of his body was made
possible by his unusual environment; his internal freedom and harmony
mirrored the external harmony he found in his wilderness home:
" 'Proud' nudity, harmony with internal nature, instinct, is closely
linked to life in the forest, harmony with external nature, closeness to
it, intimacy with animals, plants and nature's spectacle in general."[13]

White men refused the extraordinary opportunity offered by the new
continent. The challenge proved too great; Europeans recoiled in fear:
"Beware of the continent."[14] They sought to evade the wild land's powerful appeal to their "lower" natures by a lie and a murder, two aspects
of the "historical forgetfulness"[15] that is America's original sin. That
the new world's size, natural life, and inhabitants drastically exceeded
the Europeans' previous experience was simply denied. The new set-
tlers transformed this environment:

The Europeans have stripped the plains of buffalo and Indians. (57)

The Europeans drew long perpendicular lines on the plains. (58)

The Europeans have covered the plains with a thin film like a layer of paint, in which the reservations make snags. (59)

And, in terror, the exiled Europeans have begun to wait for their harvest. (60)[16]

The white man tried to reduce the wilderness's awesome power to civilized, human proportions with geometrical grids of roads and farmlands. Once they cleared the new land, they tried to treat it simply as an extension of the old (*95, 99*); European institutions were imported and a European image stamped on the new landscape. Butor describes the slavish imitation of European manners and catalogs: the endless Athenses, Oxfords, and Romes transplanted improbably in Georgia, Ohio, and Indiana.

The Indian, the *"expression of this scandalous continent,"*[17] posed as great a menace as the wild landscape he inhabited. The colonists feared him for the same reason that Chateaubriand admired him: the red man was at ease with those natural forces, external and internal, that the white man feared. The natives were either killed or, what often came to the same thing, shut off in isolated reservations. America, like Christian Europe, began with the murder of the antecedent civilization (*130*, 136). Cordova, Alabama, and Cordova, Alaska, the first two cities visited within *Mobile*, suggest a parallel between the cultural murders perpetrated in the new and old worlds. In *Génie du lieu* Butor analyzes their Spanish namesake and discusses the Moslem culture interred within Cordoba's famous mosque, now a cathedral. Garcilaso de la Vega, the great Spanish poet buried within the mosque-cathedral, links the defeated Indian and Moslem cultures: "How natural it was that Garcilaso de la Vega, the illegitimate son of a conquering captain and a princess from Cuzco, who remained profoundly Indian despite his sincere Christianity, should have chosen to be buried in this monument; how natural that it be in this city, an admirable symbol of the muffled, active persistence of a civilization, that he chose to transcribe his masterpiece, *The Royal Commentaries*, the stories he had heard in his childhood."[18] Butor's novels show buried non-Christian cultures erupting from their graves to disturb the modern European's dreams. In America the Indian reservations are *"tremendous accumulators"* from which *"spread waves of dreams."*[19] A nineteenth-century chief warned his oppressors that *"every bit of this land is sacred. . . . At night, when all sound has died away in the streets of your villages, and when you think they are empty, they will swarm with the host of those who once lived there, faithful to that sublime site. The white man will never be alone."*[20]

Mobile places slavery in the context of the European's fear of this new landscape and its Indian inhabitants. The Indian was too much at home and too much the symbol of this natural world to be easily exploited for cheap labor. The African, once wrenched from his native home, lost the primitive natural power he shared with the Indian and thus could serve the white man's economic and social purposes (*104*, 108). But the black's psychological functions were at least as important as his economic uses; he provided a protective shield between the European and his new physical and human environment: *"they served to protect us from the Indian eyes, the Indian stare, the Indian scandal. Between this land that said, 'No, you are not in Europe,' and that we tried to make into Europe, and ourselves, we stretched this black screen. . . ."*[21]

Although the white man succeeded in erecting a black wall between himself and his environment, this in turn created other problems. Despite his initial estrangement, the black, close to the earth both as a slave and as a free man, soon established "a kind of complicity"[22] with the land. The blacks in Butor's second major American text are gardeners who immediately and instinctively feel drawn to Niagara's lavish flower gardens. The Negro thus replaced the Indian as the primary symbol of the natural world and the sexual forces associated with it. *Mobile*'s dreams present an imaginary white girl's erotic fantasies about the black male: *"I smell in his odor all the odor of the woods, the swamps and the river. . . . Outside, the magnolia blossoms are opening. He lays his hand on my nightgown; it makes a great burning patch there. My heart beats in my breast, so fast. He opens his trousers."*[23] A Tennessean frankly acknowledges his fear of the black people and *"the power that lurks in their darkness."*[24] He insists on the necessity of complete segregation and warns other Americans that *"it is your civilization they threaten, they will leave almost nothing of your 'American way of life!'"*[25] These sentiments, expressed by a contemporary Southerner, have deep roots in the American past and echo concerns expressed a century and a half earlier by Thomas Jefferson (*41*, 43).

Seen against these deeply repressed fears and anxieties, the function of the official American "religion" is clear: it is yet one more barrier against the night. Butor calls attention to the dazzling whiteness of the

Washington shrines (*128*, 134) a "quasi-sacred color in the United States."[26] Similarly, the aggressively classical character of American public architecture is an assertion of the European origins of our culture. We see the subtle impact of the architectural style and color in Butor's description of blacks looking at the glaringly white reconstruction of the Greek Parthenon erected in Nashville, Tennessee (*66*, *67*; 69, 70). Elsewhere in *Mobile*, Thomas Jefferson seeks confirmation of his views on slavery and racial inequality in Homer and imperial Rome (*297*, *298*; 309, 310). American civilization, like Renaissance Christianity, manages to assimilate and reshape the classical past to its own purposes.

The two themes which I have traced, the white American's "religious" dogma and the dark fears it hides, scarcely exhaust *Mobile*, but they do define two poles around which many of its materials can be grouped. These poles are symbolized by the names of the first and last towns visited: Cordova, reminding us of Europe and the Spanish conquest of the Indian, and Buffalo, Wyoming, evoking the mythic beast venerated by the Indian and now virtually extinct. On the one hand, we see the white, European culture of Jefferson, Franklin, and Carnegie, of Ward MacCallister, Freedomland, and Clifton's Cafeteria; and on the other, the natural world and dark-skinned peoples evoked by the birds, rivers, and sea, by the litany of ancient Indian civilizations and cults.

As *Mobile* ends, there can be no doubt in which of these directions Butor's sympathies lie. This often critical descent into the American past and subconscious reveals repressed but still potent forces which hold the promise for a better future. The descent into the American night has not been in vain. The first night's descent was relatively superficial, its dreams naive and simple. The second night proves genuinely disturbing because of hidden fears it reveals. But the experience has been purging, for the next day an anonymous Tennessean can speak openly of his deepest racial, sexual fears (*253-62*, 265-69). Butor can then, during the last night's final descent, embrace the "cooling shadows"[27] and glimpse the "Aurora borealis at night. . . . the brilliant night full of stars."[28]

The nights hereafter will diminish and the days grow longer, for the book describes the forty-eight hours surrounding the vernal equinox.[29] The final chapter occurs at midnight, the beginning of another day; it opens in Eden, Wyoming, a name meant to evoke Butor's "utopian hope . . . for a truly new world."[30] The realization of this hope depends, however, upon the liberation of those dark American forces invoked by Butor at the book's close:

How long we've been waiting for you, America!
How long we've been waiting for your return! (315)

Help us, night!
O complicity!
O deaf America at night!
Terra incognita! (317)[31]

CHAPTER 7

6.810.000 litres d'eau par seconde

.

Each of *Mobile*'s chapters ends with a town or city name which is
repeated in a different state at the beginning of the next chapter. This
associative pattern carries us into Butor's next major American text.
Mobile ends in Buffalo, Wyoming; *6.810.000 litres d'eau par seconde*
(1965) describes Niagara Falls, a site very near Buffalo, New York,
where Butor spent 1962–63 teaching. As its subtitle, *étude stéréophonique*, suggests, the book is the script for a special stereophonic
performance. The text presents the voices of seventeen visitors to
Niagara Falls—old couples, bachelors, and newlyweds—which mingle
with one another and with background sounds. The voices are distributed between left and right channels, while the background sounds
and readings come from a central channel. The listener is equipped
with controls that enable him to raise or lower the sound coming
from the left or right and choose among the different voices. The
listener thus shapes the performance to his own interests. Butor extends the same freedom to the reader, offering ten different paths for
traversing the text's complex typography.

The Niagara text might be seen as an enlargement of a detail from
Mobile: an in-depth exploration of a single place which Butor believes to be of considerable importance for understanding America.
Chateaubriand, whose American books Butor greatly admires, visited
and described the falls twice, in 1797 and 1801. Butor uses these
descriptions as part of his background sounds. For Chateaubriand
and Butor the falls represent the spectacular side of American nature,
". . . the very heart, the center of this different nature."[1] Chateaubriand's description evokes the fall's violent power: "*it is less a river
than an impetuous sea whose hundred thousand torrents rush toward
the gaping mouth of a chasm.*"[2]

The falls' natural energy and spectacular beauty appeal strongly
to North Americans, drawing thousands of visitors annually. The

savage force displayed there seems to prompt the erotic desires of those it attracts, since Niagara is the most popular American honeymoon site. Many of Butor's visitors—newlyweds, middle-aged couples trying to recover their youth, matrons with their gigolos—have come to the falls to initiate or revitalize their sex lives. The many journeys of these disparate travelers are described as part of a ritual pilgrimage; the goal here, however, is not the home of the official culture honored in Washington D.C. but the center of much darker forces. These pilgrims have come to listen to "the oracle, household gods of the continent."[3] They seek the renewal that the forces of nature so powerfully revealed in these falls seem to promise; the waters will, they hope, be a "fountain of youth."[4]

The book is organized around the rhythms of the year. Twelve chapters each describe one month in Niagara's year, beginning in April and ending in March. The narrative includes three physical descents into the Niagara gorge, all with ritualistic overtones. Chapter 4 describes a journey down and behind the falls: the "pilgrims" (73, 80) separate according to sex, shed their clothes and identification, and don heavy yellow rubber cloaks in order to pass behind Bridal Veil falls. Chapters 7 and 8 recount the boat trip of a group of "penitents" (156, 157, 170; 166, 168, 171) upstream to the base of the falls. Chapter 10, entitled "The Styx," recalls the exploits of daredevils who have gone over the falls in a barrel, "a vehicle in the form of a coffin to force the door of the dead."[5]

These physical descents frame the dark journey into the subconscious at the book's center. Chapters 6 and 7 (September–October) cover the darkest hours of the night and present the couples alone in their rooms with their anxieties and fantasies. Here amidst a storm, the repressed racial fears seen in *Mobile* surface again:

> Lightning through all the streaming windowpanes,
> throws its light on the sheets,
> in the black night,
> in the black rain;
> blood;
> rain of blood,
> rain of black blood,
> rain of old black blood in the night,
> blood of the massacred returning moaning
> in the black night.[6]

Against these anxieties, the Gideon Bibles with which these rooms are equipped offer little protection (126, 135).

The couples come seeking renewal, but for most the search ends in disappointment. The middle-aged couples returning to the scene of their honeymoon find it vastly changed; the older lady and man, with their younger gigolo and mistress, experience humiliating frustration; the widow, widower, and numerous singles (including a Frenchman who resembles Butor) leave the falls as hungry for companionship as when they came. The isolation exists not only between individuals but among the couples who continually cross each others' path without speaking. Niagara's pilgrims find not rejuvenation but disillusionment and deeper loneliness. The falls prove not to be the cleansing "waters of oblivion"[7] which will wash away past failures; instead they are a "cataract of tears."[8]

Visitors journey to the falls hoping to break the normal flow of time, to find a moment of repose, and, in some cases, even to turn time back. The text's structure, while suggesting the ritual journey, also captures the frenetic pace of American life which militates against the moment of reflection the pilgrimage is meant to produce. This book's unique accelerating unities (the first chapter describes one hour, the second two hours, the third three, and so forth) mimics the river's rush to the falls and the American tourists' frenzied movement. We think of *Mobile*'s automobiles restlessly criss-crossing the continent. Here, after a night at the falls, the visitors, without quite understanding why, feel pulled back on to the highways; "For so many couples in love, now it is time to face the road again. . . . Those who had thought of staying here a few days more, but who now don't know."[9]

A pair of middle-aged Negroes stand strikingly apart amidst Niagara's emotional desolation. Despite the racial insults they suffer from whites, they remain open and tender toward each other. They contrast themselves with the whites who ignore them:

> They [a white couple] don't feel. . . .
> They don't know.
> But you know how to feel. . . .
> But you know how to feel things out.
> But you know how to figure things out. . . .
>
> They no longer know how to look at each other
> No longer know how to look at us. . . .
> There is something in them which is still looking.
> There is something in them which is stifled. . . .
> They saw us, but they probably avoided us.
> We will disturb their wedding night.[10]

These Negroes respond instinctively to nature; gardeners by trade, they revel in Niagara's flowers and, unlike the white visitors, open themselves to the night and the storm. As in *Mobile*, the dark-skinned people live closer to nature and to their deepest feelings. The Negro lady describes her husband's work-stained hands and suggests the equation of dark people–nature–sexual and emotional freedom which is so important in Butor's analysis of America: "Your hands covered with earth which you washed in order to caress me, but which smelled of soap and earth with the scent of roses above the manure, your nails still are framed in earth like young sprouts."[11]

But these blacks are a minority, and the white majority's failure is inevitable. For Butor, the falls represent not only nature's majestic power but its profanation. The frightened white man turned his back on the wilderness, creating a Europeanized America in its stead; "in the American consciousness there is a kind of fall, a Niagara which drops suddenly, and after this fall the history of the United States as a Western country begins."[12] Chateaubriand's poetic evocation of the natural splendor he found in the early nineteenth century is particularly poignant when juxtaposed with Niagara's current tawdry commercialism. *Mobile* has already shown the vulgarity of American resorts like Freedomland, but the contrast of such ugliness with one of the planet's most impressive natural wonders renders this vulgarity even more offensive. Butor is keenly sensitive to the way in which "the American mentality is written in the millions of manufactured objects"[13] that he found in his travels. Here he notes the endless post cards, plates, napkins, pillows, and ash trays which reproduce and parody the falls. Even more revealing are the miniature toilets and the pornographic salt and pepper shakers emblazoned with the falls (*15*, 22): they profane not only this natural wonder but its traditional romantic associations as well.

More is involved than the tourist promoter's greed: the garish boardwalk atmosphere is present to distract the visitor and protect him from the menacing "*chaos of the waves*."[14] The white man can be at ease with nature only after he has tamed it. The elaborately cultivated flower beds, each blossom labeled and its growing life painstakingly planned, forces nature into safe, rational patterns and dimensions. The pastel electric lights which play on the falls at night are a "homeopathic treatment,"[15] soothing and calming the raging torrent. Just as the young bride cannot show her naked lips and so paints them with bright lipstick (*15*, 22), the falls' raw, indecent power must be masked or our attention diverted. Butor offers a daring explanation of American commercial and industrial vulgarity; it results directly from America's failure to meet the wilderness's challenge:

> Thus it is because the puritan fails to extinguish in himself the appeals of this evil, of this savage, of this sensuality and of this invention, that he proclaims so loudly his success in the realms of commercial production, and that he displays his money so ostentatiously. Industry, whose enormous merit is that it permits modernity, is also corrupted. This precious mask becomes a leprosy. What was to transcend nature no longer seeks anything more than to efface, to disfigure it.[16]

Niagara Falls is one of the ugliest places in North America precisely because it is one of the most beautiful. The seductive power of this natural spectacle is too great; since it cannot be destroyed or hidden, it must be defaced.

Comparison of the Niagara text with *Description de San Marco* helps us to understand the failure we find at the falls. Both books, written within two years of each other, are done in the verbal collage manner, and both focus on specific places which are taken as microcosms of their respective cultures. Their subjects are cities located on water which are famous attractions for tourists, particularly honeymooners. And yet their moods differ radically; the sensual delight and intellectual stimulation experienced while exploring San Marco is entirely unlike the frustration and alienation found at Niagara.

A primary reason for these differences is the presence in Venice of San Marco, the building-book. The Venetians chose consciously to preserve and organize their past and to provide a meditative space where its significance could be pondered. The past at Niagara is either ignored or falsified. There is no reference to the Indian, the wilderness, or the world which antedated the white man. Niagara's "museums" offer a replica of the British crown jewels, evidence of the town's European loyalties, and mementos of earlier daredevils, which anticipate and justify the current sideshow atmosphere. The town's "architecture," a jungle of competing neon, distracts the mind into restless thrill-seeking and away from introspection or reverent contemplation of nature. Not that Venice has escaped commercialization: the babble of tourist voices runs through Butor's text. But the central portion of the book remains the description of the basilica and the transcription of its texts. At Niagara the current runs in the other direction; it is Chateaubriand's description of the falls which is thrust into the italicized background and the tourists and their entertainments which occupy center stage.

The Niagara text is a "score," the musical organization of many different elements. The final word of its terminating "Coda" is "désert," a reference to Chateaubriand's novel *Atala, ou les amours de deux sauvages dans le désert*. For Chateaubriand "désert" had a meaning close to the English "wilderness." "It in no way suggests sterility, the Sahara," Butor reminds us; "on the contrary, this wilderness is characterized by the splendor of its vegetation . . . a place human society had left intact."[17] Today, however, if "désert" is taken as a reference to modern Niagara we must translate the word as "wasteland." The text's dying note thus evokes in its two meanings both the New World's promise glimpsed by an earlier French writer and the betrayal of that hope sadly recounted by his modern successor.

"L'Appel des rocheuses"

In 1963, the year in which *Mobile* appeared, Butor also produced a shorter text on the American west. "L'Appel des rocheuses" ("The Call of the Rockies") was written to accompany photos by Ansel Adams and Edward Weston in *Réalités* (June 1962) and reworked for inclusion in *Illustrations I*. Butor ordered the photographs and their texts in the following sequence: (1) The Tetons, Wyoming; (2) Yosemite valley and falls, California; (3) Death Valley, California; (4) Death Valley and Mount Whitney. The text begins where *Mobile* ends, in Wyoming, and continues westward. We descend from the Tetons, which the *Réalités* caption tells us soar to 4,000 meters, to Death Valley, lowest point on the North American continent. The final photograph is taken from this low point but looks toward Mount Whitney, highest point in the contiguous forty-eight states. The journey thus traces once again the path of the initiatory descent.

The texts accompanying the photos in *Réalités* are of three kinds: (1) a three-paragraph *narrative* introduction in roman type on the first page describing the crossing of the Western wilderness; (2) three short *lyric* elements in italics accompanying the Yosemite photo and the two Death Valley photos; (3) short captions for the photographs, which were eliminated in the *Illustrations* version. Because of its thematic importance, I will quote the first narrative element in its entirety:

> When the pioneers were going toward the West and gold, after weeks and weeks on the plains and the prairie, they saw the large wall of rocks, peaks and forests, they knew that beyond began the deserts, the menacing immensity, the lands of wonder, and that they must resist, subsist there for weeks before reaching the other great chain and finally descending toward the Pacific.
> When the auto traveler today, after hours and hours, days of straight

highway in the interminable Midwestern farmland is greeted by the savage world within which he must thread, miniscule and alone, carefully, it is as if a gigantic breath, a wind from the depths of the ages, seizes him; he, an American, citizen of a nation so rapidly aged, finds himself renewed on the threshold of the most disquieting paradise.

When the airplane leaves the green squares whose regularity increases from Indiana to Illinois, from Iowa to Nebraska, to cross in Colorado the ultramarine mountains crowned with pearl and bathed in the surprising color of the sun constantly changing above, the young voyager is seized with vertigo: in a few moments, it seems to him, the world displays to his eyes more secrets than during years of previous studies.[18]

These three paragraphs present three parallel journeys across the Rockies into the Western desert. The three voyages, separated by modes of travel and time, share several themes. There is the contrast between the neat, geometrical Midwestern farmlands and the savage world on the other side of the mountains. Confronted by the immense, empty desert, the traveler feels insignificant, alone, and seized by vertigo. Once again, we see civilized man's anxious reaction to the wilderness. But Butor also finds this encounter enormously exhilarating and revitalizing, as we see at the end of the second voyage. The poet experiences the same mixture of fear and awe in the second lyric, set amidst Death Valley's desolate wastes:

> Your
> breath
> becomes
> such a tumult
> that you
> want
> to hold it,
> but
> you force out a cry
> that fades away.[19]

In *Illustrations*, the separate prose and poetic elements have been reworked and combined in a manner that supports and enhances the themes they express. The three voyages in the three narrative paragraphs appear simultaneously at the top, bottom, and middle of the page in ten-point roman capitals. The five verses of the first (Yosemite) lyric are introduced gradually, initially in ten-point, lower-case roman, then echoed over succeeding pages in ten-point, lower-case italic and six-point roman capitals. The gradual swelling of the text through

these echoes visually illustrates the tumult of Yosemite falls described
in the poem:

> the noise,
> the growling
> echoed
> by the sharply cut
> walls.[20]

This typographical swelling reaches its crescendo on the text's
seventh page, which is filled with seven different elements in five
different type sizes and styles. Then abruptly at the text's exact center,
the eighth of its fifteen pages, we drop into Death Valley; the page
is almost denuded of type, and we confront the vast emptiness of this
wasteland:

L'IMMENSITÉ MENAÇANTS, LE PAYS DE L'ÉTONNEMENT,

Ici

plus

un

bruit,

non,

plus

un

seul

son,

l'air

immobile.

Ici

EST SALUÉ PAR LE MONDE SAUVAGE, A L'INTÉRIEUR
DUQUEL IL LUI FAUDRA

The descent into darkness here becomes a descent into whiteness, a visual metaphor for the silence and emptiness of this last wilderness. Gradually, in the succeeding pages, the texts begin to grow again; other elements appear and swell as we move across the desert toward the mountains. As in his other texts, Butor has led us into a meeting with a central mystery, in this case the fascinating power, the "appel" of the American West which calls *Mobile*'s dreamer: "*I'm dreaming of buffalo, herds of horses, Indians of the plains, Latter-Day Saints and their trek across the states to new lands.*"[21]

"Western Duo"

The American West, more specifically the Southwest, inspired another of Butor's poems, "Western Duo," published in a limited edition by the Tamarind Lithography Workshop of Los Angeles in 1969 and collected in François Aubral's anthology of Butor's poetry in 1973. This remarkable text consists of eight sections of four stanzas each. All of the sections but the last include two stanzas in French and two in English; the final section contains three in French and one in English. The individual stanzas are simply ten nouns organized in four lines. The following eight stanzas, groups five and six, illustrate the poem's structure and content:

chevreuil	fence
courses gemmes	promontory song
cyclône herbes fantôme	ashes buffalo children
lointains gorge écorce haricots	rainbow fear canal city
wings	rivages
mesa juniper	avenir inondations
turkey weaver tribe	lavande usure soufre
history roses lava extasy	cérémonie cuir argent inconnu
granite	étendues truite autrefois tonnerre
beans pilgrims	feuilles murailles tisserands
orchards rocks mint	antennes vignes
heart meteor elk races	boucle
arbre	cliff
cuivre chandeleur	storm grass
lapins soleil glaces	ghost horizon birds
pollen torrents moufflons plateau	slopes ruins crater skin.

By piling up French and English nouns, Butor attempts to conjure the spirit of the area he explored while teaching at the University of

New Mexico in 1969–70. The American Southwest emerges in strikingly concrete detail: gorge, rainbow, mesa, juniper, and crater appear and merge with other equally vivid images. But this is a portrait of more than surfaces; familiar Butorian themes reassert themselves. Note "history," "autrefois," "fear" "fantôme," "ghost," "cérémonie," and "avenir" in the quoted stanzas; "past," "vestiges," "siècles," "légendes," "dream," "cauchemar," "solitude," and "future" appear in other stanzas. Clearly, Butor wishes to capture the historical and psychological significance of the place as well as its sensuous richness. The poem is deliberately fragmentary and partial, a preliminary incantation to prepare for the much more arduous and sustained effort to penetrate this world in *Où, Le Génie du lieu, 2.*

CHAPTER 8

Où, Le Génie du lieu, 2

The subtitle of *Où,— Le Génie du lieu, 2*—links this book to the collection of travel essays, *Le Génie du lieu*, published in 1958. The earlier volume describes those places which occupied Butor's attention during the novelistic phase of his career: Egypt, Greece, Italy, and Spain. This more recent book chronicles the non-European world upon which Butor has focused in the last decade and a half. *Où* is a composite work formed of individual narrative and poetic units written and published during the period 1959–71. Created for a variety of different situations and purposes, these pieces have been reworked to form a narrative unity. They describe a voyage between "two poles":[1] Paris, which Butor flees and to which he returns, and Sandia Mountain, New Mexico, toward which he journeys. These two distant and very different places are described in texts which recur throughout the book, sending opposed magnetic forces pulsing through the text. The Sandia Mountain poems attempt to describe the mountain in whose shadow Butor lived during his year in Albuquerque, New Mexico. More will be said about these poems later; for now it is sufficient to note that they assert the American pole, located in the Southwest, toward which he is traveling.

The remaining narrative elements are organized in the familiar pattern of withdrawal, initiation, and return. The opening and closing sections, "J'ai fui Paris" ("I fled Paris"), deal with Paris from which the protagonist, Michel Butor, departs and returns. Near the center of the work, the section "Je hais Paris" ("I hate Paris") reasserts the tension of this Parisian pole against which the traveler is reacting. The other narrative sections are:

La Boue à Seoul (The Mud at Seoul)	pp. 21–38	Day	November 1966
La Pluie à Angor (The Rain at Angor)	41–66	Day	November 1966

La Brume à Santa Barbara (The Fog at Santa Barbara)	73–100	Day and Night	March 1969
La Neige entre Bloomfield et Bernalillo (The Snow between Bloom- field and Bernalillo)	129–256	Night 9:00 P.M.– 1:00 A.M.	October 1969
Le Froid à Zuni (The Cold at Zuni)	217–388	Night 8:00 P.M.– 5:00 A.M.	December 1969

The titles indicate several unifying elements: the emphasis on mete-orological conditions and on locations in the northern hemisphere. The voyage they describe is circular—eastward from Paris to the orient, to the Pacific coast of the United States, to the American Southwest, and back to Paris. We find the same eastward movement in the fourth section's journey to Bernalillo, which lies east of Bloomfield in New Mexico. Temporally, we move forward from the narration of events in 1966 to those which occurred in 1969. Here, as in the earlier narratives, the times of darkness are emphasized, with four of the five episodes oc-curring in the fall or winter and all occurring under unfavorable meteor-ological conditions. Roughly two-thirds of the pages devoted to narra-tive elements deal with events at night. In addition, the primary series of Sandia Mountain poems, "35 vues de Mont Sandia le soir l'hiver," describes the mountain in the waning light of winter afternoon and evening. Parallel to the forward chronological movement, there is a movement backward in history. The first three sections, roughly one-third of the narrative pages of the book, treat almost exclusively the contemporary events which occur during Butor's visits to these areas. The fourth section of the book, however, has a substantial amount of material dealing with the Mormon culture, which appeared in the United States during the nineteenth century. The final section de-scribes the much older American Indian culture of the Southwest.

The Parisian sections explain the journey's motive. Like Jacques Revel and Léon Delmont, Butor is numbed by the harried pressures of urban life, and, like Delmont, he seeks a restorative in travel. The oriental chapters are the briefest in the book. Butor does not know these countries or their languages; tired and rushed, he cannot cap-ture their *genius loci*. The omnipresent Korean mud and the Cam-bodian rain remind us of the dampness and viscosity of Bleston, the city which confounded Jacques Revel. Most of the book, roughly three-quarters, is about the United States, a country Butor knows well.

In Santa Barbara, he encounters an event long anticipated in his American texts. The scene is the faculty club of the University of California at Santa Barbara, "European" with its imported Spanish ceiling and antiques, the gift of one of America's great capitalists, William Randolph Hearst. The occurrence is the dark violence feared by *Mobile*'s dreamers and those at Niagara. The night erupts with an explosion killing an old white man; black militants are suspected (95). Once again we meet the tension between official, white American culture, wealthy and Europeanized, and the latent violence seething beneath its surface.

The fourth and fifth sections are by far the longest and the most important in the book and those deserve special attention. The trip from Bloomington to Bernalillo in section four is the final leg of an automobile ride from Provo, Utah, in which the travelers cross the Rocky Mountains and descend from a peak of 9,302 feet reached at Silverton, Colorado (175). In this final segment of their trip, they cross the continental divide and go from 6,138 feet to the 4,940 feet at which Bernalillo is located. This return trip from a visit to Brigham Young University, a Mormon institution, is made against a background of texts dealing with Mormonism; it becomes a descent into this very revealing component of American culture.

Butor has long been fascinated by Mormonism; *Mobile* contains an account of its founding and early history. This interest is easily understood in the context of Butor's analysis of America. The Church of Jesus Christ of Latter-Day Saints teaches that Old Testament Israelites, led by God, came to America before the destruction of Solomon's temple and that Christ appeared to these people after his resurrection. Mormons interpret all of pre-Columbian American history and archeology in light of the *Book of Mormon*, a record of these American Israelites written by Joseph Smith. Mormonism is then a special and very obvious instance of the projection of a white, European identity on the new world. The new continent's history is Christianized, re-created according to European religious notions, with pre-Columbian America becoming Old Testament Israel. Since who we are today depends upon what we believe about our past, this "baptism" of the American past has important consequences for life in the present.

The Indian's identity is directly affected by this theft of his history. Joseph Smith, the *Book of Mormon*'s author, projects the white's traditional fear of the natural man into the past, cursing him retroactively for the temptations he arouses. The *Book of Mormon* tells how God condemned rebellious elements among these ancient immigrants, creating the dark race in the process: "And he had caused the cursing to come upon them . . . as they were white and exceeding fair and delightsome, that they might not be enticing unto my people the Lord did cause a skin of blackness to come upon them. . . . I will cause that they shall be loathsome unto thy people."[2] But Mormon attitudes toward the red man are curiously ambiguous: although cursed by God, the Indian is nonetheless a descendant of those earlier Biblical immigrants. Joseph Smith taught that the Mormons were eventually to find the lost tribes of Israel, and Brigham Young thought he had discovered the latter among the Bannock Indians of Oregon (*Mobile 46–47*, 48–49).

Mormon attitudes toward sex are equally ambivalent. Joseph Smith's *Book of Mormon* perpetuates the most repressive nineteenth-century Protestant puritanism. His deity punishes sinners swiftly and mercilessly. Butor catalogues the many ancient cities razed by this wrathful Mormon avenger: Moroni, Moroniah, Gadiadi, Zarahemla. Smith's God judges sexual transgressions with particular severity; David and Solomon's numerous wives were, we are told, "an abomination before the Lord."[3] And yet in 1852 the same Joseph Smith published a revelation instituting multiple marriages and himself married more than fifty wives (184). Brigham Young, his successor, had, at his death at the age of seventy-six, seventeen wives and forty-seven children. Butor dramatizes the conflict between these Mormon contradictions by juxtaposing on facing pages (184–85) Smith's proclamation of polygamy with the *Book of Mormon*'s account of Zarahemla's destruction for its sins. Such sexual liberty (for the Mormon men) met immediate opposition. Four of Smith's sons repudiated polygamy and founded the Reformed Church of Latter-Day Saints (184). The reaction of the dominant American Protestant culture was even more violent: Federal troops were sent to repress these multiple marriages, and in September 1857, 123 Mormon immigrants were slaughtered by American soldiers at Mountain Meadows (*Mobile 282*, 294).

In addition to the *Book of Mormon*, Butor uses portions of two other books, both French, to comment ironically on Mormonism. Guillaume Apollinaire's *La Femme Assise*, first published in 1920, recounts the adventures of Pamela, a Frenchwoman who goes to Utah with other European women and becomes a wife of a Mormon leader. Butor includes Apollinaire's descriptions of the celebration attending Brigham Young's proclamation of polygamy and of the lynching of an innocent Negro who has done nothing more serious than proclaim the black people's redemption (189–92). Butor inserts the *Book of Mormon*'s curse on the dark-skinned peoples (190) within Apollinaire's text, suggesting the cause and effect relationship between religious beliefs and racist murder. The parading of a statue symbolizing American democracy (192) ironically follows the picture of the strangled black man. Elsewhere Pamela sees a beautifully costumed Indian warrior and fantasizes flight with him (162). These romantic reveries continue *Mobile*'s theme of the erotic power exercised by the savage in the European imagination.

A visit to the Brigham Young University library collection of Marcel Schwob materials prompts Butor to introduce a text by Schwob. Butor is obviously amused at a Mormon professor's reverence for this distinctly minor French figure. The only extant letter by Schwob's mistress is described as "the pearl of great price,"[4] ironically echoing the title of a Mormon sacred text. That the letter of a young prostitute should be so regarded is all the more ironic on a campus where the students and faculty cannot drink, smoke, or wear mustaches, miniskirts, or even short-sleeved shirts (177, 197, 219). Butor quotes from Schwob's *Livre de Monelle*, a fatuous, vaguely symbolist idealization of this prostitute-lover. Monelle calls Schwob from the dark kingdom to her white kingdom. The black kingdom is dirty and scandalous (171, 192); the white kingdom is the ideal; and the red kingdom is an intermediate stage of sexual excess and destruction (199, 203) through which one passes to reach the final desired state of purity (238). These references to the black, red, and white kingdoms color Butor's text, reinforcing the racial and sexual themes already discussed.

Passages from the *Book of Mormon* suggest a mythic dimension to Butor's journey across the western mountains and desert. The most numerous and important of these references are taken from chapters eight to ten of the third Book of Nephi, which recount the effects of the crucifixion in America. Darkness comes over the earth; terrible storms assail the land, and cities crumble, as the Nephites participate metaphorically in Christ's descent into Hell. The night through which Butor travels is likened to these "Biblical" experiences by the juxtaposition of the present darkness with quotations from the Book of Nephi on page 174. References to the present barren landscape and ghost towns echo the desolation described in the *Book of Mormon*, strengthening these parallels. Butor also ironically contrasts these mythic travelers with their modern counterparts. He quotes a passage from 1 Nephi in which God gives Lehi a magic compass to guide him and his family in the desert at the very moment (172–73) Butor and his friends are taking a wrong turn that will lengthen their trip by several hours.

The mythic journey into darkness described in this section does not, however, end in Bernalillo. While the first three sections are separate and discrete, the last two sections overlap for thirty-nine pages. There is, moreover, a continuity in the times (night and early morning) and in the wintry climatic conditions. Butor establishes the strongest link, however, by juxtaposing (244–45) a stop at a diner near the end of the trip to Bernalillo with a stop at a similar diner in the course of the visit to Zuni. The travelers seem to enter the diner merely as an interlude in a single journey which is continued upon leaving.

Butor's travels to the Zuni pueblo are the final leg of the mythic voyage that is the narrative thread of *Où*. With his wife and two friends, he comes to witness the rites of the winter solstice in this desolate Indian village. Butor has traveled eastward in the dying year toward this point where the sun and the seasons are reborn. The Zuni believe this location to be the "place where everything began,"[5] the spot where man first crawled up out of the earth. The search for the *omphalos* lies at the heart of Butor's mythic quest; his heroes seek a geographical center for their lives. We recall Léon Delmont's journey to Rome, Pierre Vernier's excursion to the Greek *omphalos* in *Degrés*, and Butor's own voyage to Delphi recounted in *Le Génie du lieu*. Butor's pilgrimage to this Indian liturgical center was inevitable. We have already seen in earlier texts Butor's enshrinement of Indian culture in his vision of what America might have been. These values are all the more important in *Où*, a book whose first page bears a dedication to the Indians of New Mexico. The Zuni strikingly embody the ideal relations between man and nature and man and himself that Butor has sought in the ancient Mediterranean and American cultures. Professor Ruth Bunzel, Butor's source for much of his information about the Zuni, explains the Zuni's harmonious world view:

Of this animate universe man is an integral part. The beings about him are neither friendly nor hostile. In so far as all are harmonious parts of the whole, the surrounding forces sustain and preserve humanity in the status quo.

The sense of conflict as the basic principle of life does not dominate man's relation to the universe any more than it dominates man's relation to man. The Promethean theme—man's tragic and heroic struggle against the gods—has no place in Zuni philosophic speculation. Nor have any of the other concepts of cosmic conflicts which have always absorbed the interest of Asiatic and European philosophers and mystics, the antithesis between good and evil, or between matter and spirit. There is no Satan in Zuni ideology, and no Christ.

The world, then, is as it is, and man's plan in it is what it is. Day follows night and the cycles of the years complete themselves. In the spring the corn is planted, and if all goes well the young stalks grow to maturity and fulfill themselves. They are cut down to serve man for food, but their seeds remain against another planting. So man, too, has his days and his destined place in life. His road may be long or short, but in time it is fulfilled and he passes on to fill another role in the cosmic scheme. He, too, leaves his seed behind him. Man dies but mankind remains. This is the way of life; the whole literature of prayer shows no questioning of these fundamental premises. This · is not resignation, the subordination of desire to a stronger force, but the sense of man's oneness with the universe. The conditions controlling human affairs are no more moral issues than those, like the blueness of the sky, to which we may well be indifferent. It is an attitude singularly free from terror, guilt, and mystery.[6]

No one who has read Butor's descriptions of the tortured European and American souls can fail to understand his attraction to these people who live in peaceful unity with their world and themselves. The ceremony which we witness in this chapter is meant to assure this harmony, both spatially and temporally. These rites include an elaborate system of relations and colors (250) which "proclaims the stability of space"[7] and assures the central position of the Zuni pueblo in their cosmogony. The rites' most important function—the renewal of the seasons—is, however, temporal. The celebrants prevent the sun from disappearing forever beyond the horizon and assure the birth of another year (347). The purpose here, as in the descent of all Butor's heroes, is to lead us to that moment when past and future meet. The Zuni invoke their divine ancestors (257, 258, 292) and await the holy word which will initiate the new time (254, 297, 308).

But the quest for the *omphalos* is frustrated. The pueblo at Zuni may be the center of the Zuni world, but it can never be the center of Butor's or ours. Butor leaves before the ceremony is over and continues back to Albuquerque in the murky darkness. His companion remarks that "it is as if the sun were dead and would never again return."[8] The search must inevitably end in disappointment, for it can never lead to *the* center, but only to *a* center which then must be forsaken and the quest continued. The accent in *où* is cancelled, and *the* place becomes only another alternative. The goal of the geographical quest is the same as that on the temporal level. The descent into the past for Butor can never be the nostalgic return to a tradition which then becomes the center of our lives; it is just the reverse—the unmasking of a fraudulent notion of the past and the discovery of new alternatives for the future. Butor's narratives end, as we have seen, in the dark. He unites us briefly with our sources only to break the umbilical cord once again and force us to use our freedom in the preparation of a better future. The past is studied that it may be understood and transcended.

The forty-four poems devoted to Sandia Mountain, "35 vues du Mont Sandia le soir l'hiver" and "Neuf autres vues du Mont Sandia," reveal a movement complementary to the one seen in the narrative units.[9] This impressive granite wall rising abruptly from the New Mexico desert is one of the two poles in this voyage and has several important symbolic associations. This peak bears the name of the Sandia Indian civilization which *Mobile* (*23, 24*) informs us is the oldest in the southwestern United States, and it is thus associated with the surrounding Indian culture. But this promontory is primarily a natural rather than a human phenomenon, a fascinating and alluring physical presence mysteriously changing in the fading afternoon light. The mountain represents everything Paris is not: the cleansing American wilderness versus Europe's tired, congested cities. The final poems close the series with the theme "SOURCE" (373, 377, 382, 389), reminding us of the "fountain of youth" sought by Butor and Chateaubriand in the American desert.

The narrative units and the poems describe parallel struggles: the former recounts a physical voyage to the center of the American, Indian wilderness, the latter, the artist's effort to capture the essence of that landscape in words. The poems are penetrated and colored by the narrative journey they punctuate; echoes from the *Book of Mormon* and Zuni ceremonies appear in these lyrics. Like the prose sections, they record a ritual homage. Their titles deliberately echo Hokusai's "Thirty six and ten views of Fuji," which Butor studies in *Répertoire III.* Butor describes this series of Japanese stamps as a litany and a pilgrimage to the holy mountain.[10] A number of Butor's own poems begin with invocations to the sun god whose rays the mountain reflects: "Apollo americanus" (225), "Pautiwa" (239), "Horus" (333). Butor's titles and descriptions invite us to compare his views to Hokusai's and to see these poems as an invocation or pilgrimage to a mountain symbolizing values he wishes to honor. But these same titles point to a gap, an ironic difference between Butor's descriptions and Hokusai's: thirty-five and nine versus thirty-six and ten. The poems themselves admit their own inadequacy: "all the preceding words crumble in dust . . . it is like a more and more intense cry . . . I try once again to cast my miniscule net for this enormous prey."[11] Butor concedes the impossibility of capturing and preserving the evanescent reality of this natural phenomenon. We recall the awestruck silence Butor experienced gazing on the great desert in his Rocky

Mountain text. The quest in the Sandia Mountain poems, like that seen in the prose portions, ends in disappointment.

Butor, like Léon Delmont, will return to Paris. The voyage, however, has not been a failure. The goal is not to be reborn as an American, to trade one identity for another, but rather to multiply one's identities or perspectives. The voyage underground "brings us to the surface on the other side of the normal horizon, denounces this surface as a lie";[12] it enables us to see familiar settings from a new vantage point. Butor will return to Paris, viewing it as through the eyes of a stranger (134). The new perspective is not achieved for himself alone but for his Parisian readers. "But I will come back. To give you drink, I will come back. All my voyages draw your palpitations. And it is for you, for you, that I breathe here."[13]

European writers struggling to understand the New World have tended to produce works of two very different kinds: objective analyses of American culture, a type admirably represented by Alexis de Tocqueville's *La Démocratie en Amérique*, and highly subjective poetic evocations of a mythic America, such as Chateaubriand's *Atala* and *René*. Butor's American texts do not fall neatly into either of these categories, or rather they combine elements of both. On the one hand, his books overflow with an abundance of sociological, ethnographical and even botanical and zoological data. On the other, we are constantly aware that this material has been carefully shaped by a distinctive personal vision. The apparent randomness of *Mobile* conceals a very deliberate thematic and structural design. The main elements of this design, moreover, resemble elements we have seen earlier in the European texts. The author's own face gradually emerges within his American landscape, first as the anonymous French visitor to Niagara and then explicitly as the protagonist of *Où*.

Butor has sought in these books to evoke America's *genius loci*, to describe not only a place but the power that place occupies in his and our consciousness. Maps of a psychic space as well as a physical one, these texts must be subjective and poetic as well as empirical and analytical. I have insisted on Butor's divergent purposes and methods in order to explain how a reader, particularly an American reader, might properly react to these texts. We might fairly object that certain features, sexual repression and the businessman's greed for instance, seem overdrawn. (We ought, however, to keep in mind that Butor, who continually refers to white Americans as "Europeans", inculpates the Old World fully as much as the New.) To see such overemphasis only on the sociological level without proceeding to the poetic level is, I believe, a mistake. Butor necessarily strengthens certain themes to create structural girders that will give his American texts internal coherence and join them to his other works. Butor's American trilogy, despite the radical heterogeneity of its materials, achieves these goals admirably. It extends Butor's historical schema into the modern American Age and presents a remarkably comprehensive view of our culture. The first volume provides an overview and reveals the contradictory pressures contending within the American psyche. The second book, situated in the Northeast, focuses primarily on the white European's commercialism, while the third, located at the opposite, Southwestern end of the country, explores the darker forces of native American culture. Butor's three American texts, taken as a group, provide us with an unusually imaginative, and technically innovative portrait of contemporary America.

CHAPTER 9

Intervalle

Intervalle might well have been subtitled *La Modification II*. The idea must surely have occurred to the author of the *Répertoire* and *Illustrations* series, for *Intervalle* seems a conscious attempt to return, in 1973, to the situation and themes of Butor's most famous novel. Like Léon Delmont, Marc, a middle-aged Parisian trapped by his bourgeois family, dreams of beginning a new life with Adrienne, a young widow he encounters on a train trip. They meet, privately consider escaping to Venice, and then part and return to their monotonous lives. *La Modification* reveals the magnetic attraction of Rome in the life of the modern European; *Intervalle*, the mythic power of Venice. Both books unmask an uncritical submission to these myths as forms of self-evasion. While the earlier book focuses on this dilemma's cultural roots in the past, *Intervalle* explores its contemporary context and tries to provide an opening on a future free of such self-deception.

Description de San Marco had already shown Venice's rich sensual beauty, and the city evokes similar associations here in Marc and Adrienne's reveries. Indeed, Marc has even read Butor's book, and quotations from it and a Venetian guidebook weave their way through his interior monologues. An art-lover married to a woman bored by museums, Marc dreams of Venice's art treasures. Adrienne yearns for the city's warm sun, sea, and canals, so unlike her drab, native Montbrison, ironically touted as the "Venice of central France."[1] For each, the other is associated with this dream city: Marc's name recalls Venice's patron saint, and Adrienne's interest in a Venetian book first draws Marc's attention to her. Both of these individuals habitually travel the train route from Paris to Saint-Etienne. They meet at Lyon, the point at which it would be possible to break their itinerary and initiate a new one—a voyage to Venice.

But they do not break out. So deeply ingrained are their inhibitions that they separate without even discussing their dreams. Butor explains their failure by placing it in a context of nineteenth- and twentieth-century texts that interact with the two interior monologues. Passages from Gérard de Nerval's *Sylvie* and his *Voyage en Orient* comment on the romantic attraction of an ideal lover and the equally romantic voyage of escape. Marc has read both of these works, and his memories of them are triggered by a comic strip version of the *Voyage* which he reads in *France-Soir*. The Nerval quotations which recur throughout the text are thus echoes in Marc's memory.

Adrienne bears the name of the beautiful and mysterious woman who captivates the hero of *Sylvie*. Gérard, Nerval's protagonist, meets a beautiful noblewoman during a country dance and hears her sing a simple ballad about an imprisoned princess. Enchanted, Gérard kisses her and crowns her with flowers. But Adrienne, the captive of a jealous father, disappears as quickly and mysteriously as she appeared. Haunted by this memory, Gérard searches for Adrienne for years, abandoning hope only when he learns she has entered a convent. The young widow Marc meets in the depot waiting room resembles her Nervalian namesake in several ways. She appears abruptly in Marc's life and is the captive of a vindictive mother-in-law. Both women are associated with romantic, mist-draped lands: Valois, "that foggy land"[2] of Nerval's heroine and "the Venetian winter, the fog"[3] of her modern counterpart. Most important, both Adriennes symbolize romantic, ideal love unattainable in the quotidian world. The *Sylvie* passages occur in the first half of *Intervalle* (through Chapter 16) during the period when Marc seriously considers a break with his past life. These passages suffuse this section with a romantic aura which suggests the unrealistic character of Marc's plans.

Selections from *Voyage en Orient* continue the Nervalian tone and establish parallels between Marc and Adrienne's projected trip to Venice and Gérard de Nerval's travels to the Greek island of Cythera (59). Butor has selected his passages from chapters 15 and 16 of the "Introduction" to *Voyage*. Nerval has earlier described his hopes for this journey. He recalls Watteau's famous painting *Embarcation pour Cythère* and Francesco Colonna's sixteenth-century, Neo-platonic account of Polyphile and Polia's love consummated at Venus's temple on Cythera. Nerval is, in short, a pilgrim to the shrine of ideal love. The Nervalian passages used by Butor recount key events on that voyage and their disillusioning consequences. Butor does not use these passages in the order in which they occur in the original, and this rearrangement significantly affects their meaning within *Intervalle*. The following table contrasts the sequence of these passages in Butor's text and their order in the Pléiade edition of Nerval's works.[4]

Intervalle		_Voyage en Orient_	
sequence	page	sequence	page
1 (_F–S_)	11	2	89
2 (_F–S_)	16	3	89
3 (_F–S_)	16	5	90
4 (_F–S_)	19	7	90
5 (_F–S_)	25	8	90
6 (_F–S_)	108	9	90
7	133–34	4	90
8	147	10	91
9	148	6	90
10	156	11	91
11	161	12	91
12	161	1	74–75
13	161–62	13	93

A comic strip version of _Voyage_ in a copy of _France-Soir_ purchased by Marc introduces these selections into the text. The first six passages (indicated by _F–S_) are quoted from this newspaper. In passages one through five, Nerval explains how on the island of Syra he took rest in the shade of a windmill and met a woman who spoke to him of a lovely young girl. These selections appear early in _Intervalle_ and correspond generally with the romantic theme and tone of the _Sylvie_ passages quoted in the same section. The sixth passage, also from _France-Soir_, alters this tone as the old lady leads Gérard into an ominously sordid cabaret. This selection appears in _Intervalle_'s chapter 23, well after it has become clear that Marc and Adrienne will not succeed. The changed tone thus suits this section's altered psychological atmosphere.

Butor places the comic strip version in context by inserting seven additional passages from Nerval's original, not published by the newspaper. These passages considerably expand the causes of Nerval's disappointment and accompany Marc and Adrienne's renunciation of their hopes in the final chapters. Selection seven, which ought to have followed three but which was omitted by _France-Soir_, sadly contrasts the ancient glory of these islands with their contemporary decrepitude. Eight and ten make explicit the old woman's base intentions (she is a procuress soliciting for a prostitute) and Gérard's sad refusal. The images of the hangman and the tomb in the following two passages, numbers twelve and thirteen, vividly evoke Nerval's bitter despair at the death of ideal, classic beauty and love:

As we passed the coast, I saw a small monument vaguely outlined against the blue of the sky and seated atop a rock, which seemed the still standing statue of some protective divinity . . . but upon coming closer we saw more clearly this object which drew travelers' attention to this coast. It was a gallows.[5]

Egypt is a vast tomb; that is the impression that the beach at Alexandria made on me, with its ruins and hillocks offering to the eyes scattered tombs on a land of cinders. Shades draped in bluish shrouds move among this debris.[6]

The twelfth passage (the first quoted above) actually occurs much earlier in *Voyage* than any of the other passages, but one sees immediately why Butor has moved it here. The gallows on the isle of love and the tombs in the thirteenth passage provide the full stop to Marc and Adrienne's hopes of romantic escape. The Nervalian passages make explicit once again the association of sensual release and the ancient pagan world. They also reassert the impossibility of a naive escape into this world. The same forces which confounded Léon Delmont also defeat Marc and Adrienne. Constrained by culturally induced inhibitions, they cannot even discuss their hopes. Butor concedes that there was once a time when "Venus' island was not nailed with a gallows,"[7] but that day ended with the advent of Christianity. He poses a rhetorical question: "Is there today a single region where the shadow, the stench of some cross does not prohibit our gaze?"[8] If we have followed his cultural analysis this far, we already know the negative answer.

The failure of these would-be lovers is thus rooted in the historic cultural problems with which we are familiar from other Butor texts. But more than for any previous characters, Marc and Adrienne's situation is embedded in a concrete contemporary political and social context. Political references are not entirely absent in Butor's earlier work. *Réseau aérien* (1962) describes the return from Saigon of a French colonist haunted by the suffering he and his countrymen had inflicted there. *Illustrations II* (1969) includes a description of a Vietnamese monk's self-immolation in protest of the Nhu regime and a portrait of Berlin divided by the Cold War. Butor has also been a signatory and contributor to various political protests by literary figures during the sixties. His earlier analyses, however, emphasized the historic causes rather than the immediate political symptoms of our problems.

Marc and Adrienne meet in February 1968. Selections from the *Le Monde* and *France-Soir* that they and others in the waiting room read on that day suggest the contemporary context, "thus putting the information in perspective."[9] News of the Tet offensive in Vietnam reminds us that the forces which pointlessly sacrificed Adrienne's husband in the Algerian War and which have warped her mother-in-law continue at large in the world. References to tensions between Arabs and Israelis and between the Czechs and Russians call our attention to the divided world in which we live. French labor problems and the suicide of a French worker assert the same fact on a more local level. The North African workers, soldiers, priests, and nuns who wander through the room where Marc and Adrienne wait make the abstract forces described in the text even more physically immediate. This is Marc and Adrienne's prison.

Intervalle is a book about travel in which no one moves. It restates and amplifies one of the main themes of *La Modification*: the denunciation of the naive equation, travel = change. Léon Delmont mistakenly equates a mere physical reorientation, the substitution of Rome for Paris, with moral and intellectual modification. The physical voyage, as Butor has shown us so often, can and should be the occasion for a deeper voyage of self-discovery; but, in many cases, it is simply an excuse for self-evasion. Delmont finally realizes that his attempt to flee his problems was foolish and that the only true change is of one's consciousness. Marc's and Adrienne's travel plans are doomed for the same reasons, although they are only dimly aware of this fact at the book's conclusion. *Intervalle* and the essay "Le Voyage et l'écriture" ("Travel and Writing"), first published in 1972, analyze the role of travel in our culture and thus provide a valuable coda to one of the guiding themes of Butor's work.

Travel for most of us today means tourism: "Travel, a word repeated thousands of times in the streets, in advertising, it is terribly seductive. It draws us into the travel agency."[10] The walls of the Lyon-Perrache railway station are blazoned with travel posters whose seductive appeals echo through Marc's and Adrienne's interior monologues. Travel thus understood represents a cleansing escape away from one's problems into a new, hopefully regenerative landscape: "it is the beach, or the ski slope. Leave your cares behind! Escape!"[11] Seen from this perspective, Marc's and Adrienne's dreams of abandoning their jobs and families and fleeing to Venice are a sophisticated form, more serious in its potential consequences, of the romantic escape promised by the Club Mediterranée.

Butor deliberately contrasts this notion of the voyage with Nerval's more authentic example. The Romantics—Chateaubriand, Lamartine, Gautier, Nerval, and others—were great travelers and travel writers.

The voyage was for them, as for Butor, essentially a pilgrimage: "the voyage to . . . an oracular site; one brings a question and awaits an answer, the healing of the body or the soul. The holy place stands apart amidst the secular world; it is a window on paradise. Then the pilgrimage becomes a voyage to places which speak, which speak of our history and ourselves."[12] The ideal nineteenth-century itinerary included Rome, Athens, and Jerusalem, our cultural well-springs, the places which speak most revealingly to us about ourselves. Chateaubriand's *Itinéraire de Paris à Jérusalem* represents for Butor a classic instance of this type of cultural pilgrimage. Nerval, however, deliberately avoided this famous trio of cities and chose instead three intermediate sites: Constantinople, Beirut, and Cairo. Nerval believed that the major centers had been distorted and corrupted; he therefore felt that he had to visit other sites where he could view these primary sites from another perspective. Only by standing back could one sense the distortions and see their powerful effect on men's minds: "Chateaubriand's pilgrimage is a voyage in history, Gérard's in the distortion of history."[13]

We now see the full significance of Butor's use of Nerval in this book: Chateaubriand's voyage is the archetype behind *La Modification*'s itinerary, but Nerval's *Voyage* is the model for the route studied in *Intervalle*. The former compares Paris and Rome by placing them at opposite ends of the same journey; *Intervalle* studies the relationship between France and Venice by means of a trip between Paris and another French city, Saint-Etienne. Butor reveals Venice's mythic power by measuring the magnetic attraction it exerts in the minds of a Parisian and a citizen of Saint-Etienne at that point, Lyon, where the railroad lines between these cities intersect with the line to Venice.

The seductive appeal of Venice is directly proportional to the antipathy engendered by the other two cities. Adrienne feels trapped in Saint-Etienne, a dreary industrial city known, among other things, for its armament industry. (Butor acknowledges that had he known the city earlier he would have used it rather than Manchester for *L'Emploi du temps* [60].) Although Marc loves Paris, he cannot enjoy the city because of his imprisonment in a tiny apartment and a job he detests. But Marc and Adrienne cannot move to a new life in Venice until they first travel inward and face honestly the problems which are driving them away from their old lives.

Butor wishes not only to describe our dilemma but also to find an entry into a ·solution. The key in this instance resides in the redirection of those energies wasted by escapist reverie toward a forthright examination of the problem. The voyage and literature both play crucial roles in this exploration. Traveling, reading, and writing are for Butor closely related activities. His trips are, as we have seen, essentially the deciphering of a site or series of sites, an act of reading, which then becomes the subject of an act of writing. Our reading of the resulting text enables us to share the initial voyage and discovery. Butor hopes that changing the ways we read his book, a text, will also change the ways we read our cultural situation, our context. This is more than merely sympathetic magic: both activities require the substitution of a free and creative intelligence for the passive evasion of self-awareness.

The danger to be avoided is escapist literature, a literary form corresponding to escapist travel. The seductive appeal of such reading resides in what Butor calls the "mythology of whiteness." He explains that: "The escape that it permits from the wounding, pressing, dark, hatred-filled daily world makes reading a purificatory ceremony. . . . The elsewhere that the book gives us appears to us across the page as penetrated by whiteness, baptized. Sometimes the refusal of the world as it is, the discouragement before the difficulties of its transformation, becomes so strong that the reader prefers to remain suspended in this whiteness, tranquil at last."[14] Reading becomes dangerous when we seek to hide in the soporific "whiteness" that it offers. Butor seeks in his writing to provide an antidote to this narcotic. To see how he has attempted to do this in *Intervalle* we must pursue the relationship between travel, reading, and writing a bit further. Reading is travel in two senses: when we open a book we are transported mentally into an *imaginary space*, the book's setting; we also cross a *physical space* as our eyes follow the movement of the words across the page and through the book.

Butor expands the imaginary space of his basic narrative. Not only does he invite us into the Lyon-Perrache station, his setting, and the Venice which exists in Marc's and Adrienne's minds (these are the fundamental *données* of a sentimental love story), but he extends this world spatially and temporally by the inclusion of texts not normally deemed appropriate. *Le Monde* and *France-Soir* set these dreams of flight against the background of contemporary political problems— Vietnam, the Middle East, labor troubles, and the like. Butor also includes the Nerval selections to correct the escapist, comic-strip version of *Voyage* and to send us to a work he obviously regards as a neglected masterpiece. Nerval's *Voyage* provides a valuable cultural commentary on the theme of flight. Anyone fleeing the real world into Butor's fiction finds himself led back into the very culture from which he would escape.

Intervalle's fictional space expands not only outward but inward, exploring the creative consciousness of its author. Butor deliberately breaks the mimetic illusion and reminds us that the text is an artifact, the creation of human intelligence. He includes extracts from three separate journals, representing three stages of writing and revision, as well as additional *autocritiques*. We are invited into the writer's study both as spectators and as collaborators who are encouraged to continue the process of reflection and creation which this book has begun. Butor urges his readers: "*do it yourself too*" (59); "*try my own ways to find your ways*" (64); "*try your own way to find my ways*" (73).

The expansion of the fictional space of *Intervalle* is made possible by Butor's treatment of the book's physical space. The book's un-orthodox typography permits the juxtaposition of its many different elements: Nerval, newspapers, Butor's journals, and the story of Marc and Adrienne: "textual leap-frog, that's my real novel."[15] The book's unusual physical format also serves the further purpose of interrupting the eye in its journey, deliberately sullying the mythical whiteness to which we would retreat. The reader's eye must travel up and down, backwards and forward, in order to make the necessary connections. No reading of *Intervalle* is possible other than an *active* and a *creative* one.

Intervalle, of all Butor's texts since *Degrés*, is the work which most resembles a novel. There are characters and a romantic intrigue in many ways like that of *La Modification*. But these similarities with *La Modification* set in relief important differences, such as textual collage and the exploration of electronic media, and remind us of the distance Butor has traveled in the postnovelistic phase of his career. *La Modification* contested the linear notion of *time*, but it did so within the traditional notion of the book; *Intervalle* contests the linear notion of the *book* as well.

The goal, as always for Butor, is greater human awareness and freedom. Butor remains hopeful of a future when there will be "neither soldiers nor nuns, nor a waiting room at Lyon-Perrache." If such a day arrives it will be because the book, transformed by experiments such as these, "will in some way have contributed to the abolition of today's horrors."[16]

The Future and Its Literature

We have followed Butor as he traced the roots of our present dilemma deep into the past. But Butor also faces forward: he tells us, "I am preparing a different civilization, a different life."[17] Butor's interest in the future, seen as early as his first novel in the Léonard group's conversations, has asserted itself with particular strength in the last seven years. Butor's recent study and use of Charles Fourier, the late eighteenth- and early nineteenth-century Utopian thinker, is a clear indication of this interest. Fourier's name first appears in *Passage de Milan*'s futurological conversations and resurfaces in several passing references in the sixties.[18] In 1970 Butor published *La Rose des vents, 32 rhumbs pour Charles Fourier* as well as a shorter poem "La Politique des charmeuses" and an essay devoted to this thinker.[19] Butor also used Fourier's ideas to give a unique, Utopian interpretation to Beethoven's Diabelli Variations in his 1972 *Dialogue* with this musical composition. *Intervalle* raises the hope of a better future and explicitly reminds us that literature will play a substantial role in its creation. These speculations raise two important questions: what shape would Butor have the future take, and how can literature hasten the arrival of this new society?

The specific contents of the future which Butor would wish for us are not spelled out in the same detail as his historical schema of the past, but we can outline a number of key ideas about the future. First, man must be liberated from those forces which presently suppress and divide him. The primary sources of division and repression within our culture have been identified in Butor's earlier texts: they are capitalism and Christianity. Our capitalist, imperialist social order traps Horace Buck and the nameless North Africans of *Degrés* in degrading and alienated labor. Even the seemingly affluent suffer: Léon Delmont is filled with self-loathing by his service to an economic empire in which he does not believe. All are caught in a system which constricts both their actions and their feelings.

Christianity supports and intensifies this intellectual and instinctual repression: "the installation of Christianity with its furious sexual censorship has been a means of preserving the reality of slavery while doing away with the name."[20] Rigid Christian sexual taboos constrain and redirect the libido toward the purposes determined by the social and economic system. The close relationship between religious and socioeconomic power emerges clearly in *La Modification*, where Henriette and Signor Scabelli own joint title to Léon Delmont's soul. The same forces that repress us, divide us. Capitalism and imperialism erect barriers between the white, developed peoples and the colored races and, within the white world, between economic classes. The religious opposition of Christian versus pagan reinforces the racial and economic barriers between the West and the rest of the world.

Butor would banish capitalism and Christianity from his new order. *Intervalle* looks forward to a time when soldiers, priests, and nuns have disappeared from the Lyon depot, and "La Politique des charmeuses" imagines an epoch when capitalist profiteers and manipulators will have been long forgotten. Butor's Beethoven *Dialogue* contains a prophetic vision of the eventual destruction of our present religious and social system. Butor links Beethoven's thirty-three Diabelli variations to Fourier's thirty-two stages in social history and includes in his gloss of the climactic thirty-second variation the legend of Adoniram, taken from Gérard de Nerval's *Voyage en Orient*. Adoniram, architect of Solomon's temple, descends to the center of the earth and meets his ancestors, the ancient pagan gods dispossessed by Jehovah. From them he hears a prophecy of the eventual overthrow of the reigning deity and his secular underlings: "the indefatigable army of laborers . . . and the troop of workers, of thinkers, will one day overthrow the blind power of the kings, Adonai's despotic ministers."[21] Butor, who has so often shown us the paradoxical relationship of past and future, cannot have missed the ironic fact discovered by Adoniram: man must go back to the pre-Judeo-Christian past to find the inspiration for his new order.

Adoniram's revolt is primarily negative; *La Rose des vents* spells out a vision of the future in more positive terms. Charles Fourier foresaw thirty-two periods in human history but described only the first nine. Butor, following Fourier's own guidelines, has attempted to complete this description. It would, however, be a mistake to take *La Rose des vents* as a literal prediction of the future or as a serious political program. Fourier's works combine astonishing political and social insights with the purest fantasy (strange animals walk the earth; the sea turns to lemonade). Fourier, Butor admits, "spreads before our eyes, in his cosmological digressions, an immense and burlesque world, with no concern for proof or verisimilitude."[22] Butor completes Fourier's vision in the only manner possible—with Fourier's own mixture of high seriousness and humorous fantasy. Fourier's vast temporal architecture abounds in elaborate symmetries and poetic correspondences; Butor obviously delights in this formal play at least as much as in Fourier's ideas. Still, Butor clearly identifies with the basic spirit of Fourier's program, and he urges us at the end of "La Politique des charmeuses" to "*votez* CHARLES FOURIER." The key metaphor is the compass card (*rose des vents*) of Butor's title: Fourier points the general direction the future must take.

At the heart of Fourier's complicated vision lies a very simple but absolutely revolutionary idea: man's natural passions are fundamentally good. Earlier social thinkers sought to restructure society to suit man. Rather than repress man's passions, Fourier's ideal society would encourage these passions and then organize them in socially useful combinations. Man's desires, including his sexual desires, would under Fourier's regime be liberated and intensified. Butor foresees under this program the glorification of man's senses and predicts the discovery of entirely new colors, tastes, and scents. The appeal of this program, which Roland Barthes calls an "eudémonisme radical,"[23] for Butor is immediately obvious. From the Ralon brothers to Marc and Adrienne, his characters stifle their deepest desires and suffer the tragic consequences. Butor's future would enable them to discover and enjoy their true selves.

Fourier's dream is also universalist. A precursor of Marx, he would eliminate private property and emancipate all classes, races, sexes, and age groups. Mankind would be joined in a system that would be not merely global but eventually interplanetary. A particularly striking example of these plans for harmonious unity and sensual freedom is the interplanetary erotic opera. Butor explains how in this unique art form lovers on distant planets would be joined through the use of intermediaries. The barrier between participant and spectator would be abolished, and the audience would also join in these communal, sensual experiences. The vision is Fourier at his most fantastic, but its attraction for Butor, whose texts show us a hopelessly divided world, is clear.

Butor is, finally, neither a politician nor a social philosopher, but an artist. Thus he is concerned about developing new literary forms for the future. Indeed, the writer can best fulfill his revolutionary responsibilities by working to transform the structures we use to organize our experience: "The book is so central in our civilization that, if one can only change them correlatively, it is probably the best point of attack. . . . To write is the best action."[24] Since the early sixties Butor has directed his literary experiments first toward transforming the book and then toward creating literary forms which go beyond the book. *Description de San Marco*, the American texts, and the numerous limited-edition *illustrations* which combine poetry and art visually enrich the traditional book form. The operatic libretto "Votre Faust" and the Niagara *étude stéréophonique* provide the verbal texts for multi-media theatrical performances. These new literary forms aim at the same goals of greater personal freedom and cultural unity that Butor has sought in his Utopian discussions.

Intervalle, Butor's most recent narrative, illustrates the nature of his multi-media experiments and the objectives they seek. Although the book may be read as a novel, it is actually a visionary *ciné-roman*, the verbal outline for an electronic event that exceeds the capacity of any existing theatrical facility. The text calls for six different projectors and screens, a series of television monitors with an array of different videotapes, and stereo headsets with a choice of channels. The earlier "open" novels and texts invite our participation; "Votre Faust," Butor's operatic libretto, even asks the audience to vote at key junctures in the plot. *Intervalle* would, in performance, go much further: Butor deliberately overloads the viewer's circuits, *forcing* him to make choices of what he will see or hear, involving him directly in the structuring of his own aesthetic experience. He would awaken his audience from their passive torpor, stimulate them to think out the implications of the situations presented, and encourage them to exercise their freedom in choosing solutions.

Butor would awaken his audience both intellectually and sensuously. Dulled by centuries of Cartesian rationalism, literature has ceased to be a sensuous experience for us. We no longer see or hear the word; it has become a transparent symbol through which we pass toward a concept. Butor wishes to restore to literature the visual beauty of the illuminated manuscript and the music of oral poetry. His short film "Lautréaumont" projects words as well as images on the screen and combines them with poetry on the sound track. He sees in the electronic media the way not to replace the word but to enrich it: "Then will triumph that revolution begun by Gutenberg, which we see that four centuries have only haltingly begun."[25]

Butor envisions spectacular literary events of the future that would join men all over the world with one another and with their past. Special theaters utilizing printed texts, electronic projection, and recordings would be linked globally. Audiences would enjoy all the pleasures of the eye and the ear and would be able to interact with others in remote areas of the planet. Satellites, through the miracles of electronic miniaturization, could be equipped with the riches of the world's great libraries, film archives, and museums. Individuals could draw on these resources through private consoles for use during these public events or for their own personal explorations.[26] In the adaptation of the new technology to serious literary purposes, Butor sees tools with which we can construct a freer, more conscious and integrated civilization. He asks us to imagine "those future cities where, at the principal intersections unique building-instruments, . . . would play or you yourself could play, irreplaceable counterpoints invading all your senses, where world history, human will power would be reflected, discovered differently in each place, where the variety of our mental landscape would be augmented by an illuminating dimension."[27]

Butor's futurological speculations both on the structure of society and on its literature are vague and suggestive rather than detailed and programmatic: they are intended as stimuli for further thought and experimentation. We note many of the same qualities in the future projected here and in the classic Mediterranean and Indian cultures excavated earlier. The ancient Golden Age and the future Utopia function in the same way for Butor: both ideal societies, equally unattainable in our present world and situated at opposite ends of history, serve as valuable background surfaces against which we can view and judge the present. Contrasts and alternatives, they set in relief our present failures by the brilliance of their ideal beauty: "The movement of poetic thought, initially a return to a lost past, will be indefinitely sent further, such that it can find rest only beyond this world and time, 'anywhere out of the world,' in a utopia or a 'uchronia' . . . in that outside of history that will present itself precisely as 'that which we desire.' This reminiscence and this nostalgia suddenly open on our future. Thus poetry, critic of present life, proposes to us its transformation."[28]

Conclusion

Michel Butor: Modernist-Postmodernist

"History," Stephen Dedalus complains in James Joyce's *Ulysses*, "is a nightmare from which I am trying to awake." Stephen's lament voices the concern of an entire literary generation, for the problematic relationship of the present to the past lies at the heart of international literary modernism. Butor's own Janus-like stance between past and future, to be properly understood and appreciated, must be placed in the context of the important questions raised by the modernist masters.

Flaubert captured the nineteenth century's guiding theme when he wrote to Louise Colet that the leading characteristic of their age was its historical sense.[1] In the wake of the French Revolution and the Napoleonic period, it became impossible to credit the Christian and neoclassical notion of an immutable human nature frozen in a divinely ordained social order. The dramatic political and social reversals of this period drove nineteenth-century man to two inescapable conclusions: human existence is conditioned by the unique social and cultural environment in which it is embedded, and this environment is mutable. Human existence appeared, in the dawn of the early century's new freedoms, to be evolving upward toward an even more glowing future. This historical vision of the world as process colored every aspect of late eighteenth- and nineteenth-century life and thought: Hegel conceived the world of spirit as dynamic and evolving; Marx did the same for economic and social relations, Lyell for geology, and Darwin for biology.

The European novel appeared and grew contemporaneously with the developing historical consciousness. The new genre was born out of the need for an expansive form which could express these complex new social relationships and capture their evolution over a period of years. "The novel was the diachronic form of a diachronic age."[2] Dickens, Balzac, Stendhal, Dostoevsky, and Tolstoy show us ordinary individuals caught up in the sweep of this vast historical tide. Their novels, mimicking their historical model, move in a linear fashion, chronologically from past to present. But the vision darkened. Napoleon III offered a bitter parody of the greatness promised by his famous namesake. The new industrial masters proved even more abusive than the nobility they had replaced. Social dislocation, labor troubles, and the growth of anarchism—World War I climaxed this whole dismal spiral. The engine of progress became a pulverizing dynamo; Clio became Medusa. Literature, beginning with the naturalists of the 1880s, came gradually to reflect this gloomier perspective. The modernists, the unusually brilliant group of writers who emerged internationally during the *anni mirabilis* 1910–30, inherited this dispiriting vision.

The modernist met the terror of history by seeking different ways to describe man's experience in time. They replaced or supplemented the historical model of a horizontal line, which now appeared to be pointed dangerously downward, with two temporal concepts, which may be represented by a vertical line and a circle. The vertical line symbolizes the subjective interior experience of temporal depth which moves according to patterns very different from those of external time measured by clocks. The Romantics had already sensed the fullness of the unique instant of intellectual or emotional intensity, but Bergson gave this intuition its clearest and most influential philosophical formulation. Proust, Joyce, Woolf, and Faulkner developed techniques such as chronological dislocation, interior monologue, and stream of consciousness to render this time sense novelistically.

The surrealists pursued these subjective experiences even further into dreams and the unconscious. They sought, as André Breton explained in the Second Surrealist Manifesto, to reach that *point suprême* where opposites fuse, and past and future merge. Kafka, the expressionists, and the absurdists turned this subjective experience inside out. The vertical descent continues; as with the surrealists, the moment is wrenched from its historical context and rendered with an absolute scorn for clock-time logic. But the intensely subjective experience of the dream or mental derangement is cast back as an objective, public experience. History becomes quite literally a nightmare from which we cannot awake.

The circle symbolizes both recurrence and eternity. In refuting Hegel's historicism, Nietzsche formulated the notion of eternal return. The transformations described by historians are, he insisted, only apparent and superficial: nothing changes; all things recur. Pursuing this insight, the modernists structured their narratives on ancient myths; Odysseus, Orpheus, and Absalom appeared in modern dress. If one descends far enough into the psyche, Freud and Jung had argued, one meets the eternal archetypes incarnated in myth. At this point the vertical and circular times merge, and our deepest personal memories open onto a communal experience outside of history.

The modernists often forswore the novel's temporal and spatial freedom and organized their narratives around the circular rhythms of the day or year: Joyce's day in Dublin, Virginia Woolf's in London, Hermann Broch's final hours with Vergil. Myth and the unities are neoclassical devices; to understand their modern reappearance we have only to consider the metaphysical assumptions upon which they traditionally rested. Human nature is unchanging, the Renaissance believed, and the artist's task is to express it in its essential aspect *sub specie aeternitatis*. Ancient myth can therefore speak to the present, and a single day can be extracted from a life or an epoch, like a thin section cut from a muscle tissue whose striations are uniform throughout.

Unsympathetic critics sensed the dangers in the modernist withdrawal from history. Georg Lukacs feared that this emphasis on the private and subjective experience "must deprive literature of a sense of *perspective*."[3] The modernists' subjectivism risked obscuring vital connections between man and his particular environment and thus threatened man's power to act on that environment. Philip Rahv, disturbed by the modernists' attraction to myth, warned that "the fear of history is at bottom the fear of the hazards of freedom. In so far as man can be said to be capable of self-determination, history is the sole sphere in which he can conceivably attain it."[4]

There can be no question of the modernists' profound antipathy for the era in which they were entrapped nor of their deep yearning (counterbalanced by other pressures) to extract themselves from history. But, for the most part, the novelists' attempt to retreat from history did not succeed and was not meant to succeed. The reappearance of mythical figures in modern dress does not manage to annihilate the intervening centuries; on the contrary, the ironic gap between Odysseus and his modern Joycean counterpart only dramatizes the historical distance between Homer's time and our own. Despite the elaborate mythical patterning (Homer, the Mass, the unities), the gross immediacy of Joyce's naturalistic detail overflows and exceeds these structures; Bloom, Stephen, and Molly remain absolutely and irretrievably rooted in the nightmare of Dublin, 16 June 1904.

The modernists' response to history must be seen not so much as a withdrawal but as an attempt to *reculer pour mieux sauter*: not flight but a search for a new perspective from which the modern situation and the forces shaping it can be seen globally. Stephen Spender, looking back at the literary generation of which he had been a part, writes that "the confrontation of the past with the present seems to me the fundamental aim of modernism. The reason why it became so important was that, in the early stages of the movement, the moderns wished to express the *whole* experience of modern life."[5] The desire to frame a portrait of the modern world as a whole situation is at bottom an epic ambition. Flaubert had already expressed in 1854 a nostalgia for writers like Homer and Rabelais, whose works were "encyclopedias of their epoch";[6] this desire for an inclusive, synthesizing artistic vision was to become a guiding motif of the modernist era. Stephen Dedalus proclaimed at the end of *A Portrait of the Artist as a Young Man* his (and Joyce's) hope of creating the "uncreated conscience of his race." *Ulysses* is the ironic product of that ambition. Ezra Pound committed himself to the same epic task when he described his *Rock Drill Cantos* as "the tale of the tribe . . . it is their purpose to give the true meaning of history as one man has found it."[7]

These efforts were analogous in scope and intent to the great nineteenth-century sagas of Balzac, Stendhal, Tolstoy, and Dostoevsky, with the important difference that the historical model upon which the nineteenth-century masterpieces were grounded was now inadequate. The nineteenth-century paradigm, based on Hegel's God Who is History, assumed that meaning was immanent in chronological succession, a notion no longer tenable. The historical perspective also emphasized external political and social change, obscuring more subtle intellectual and moral changes; it could not adequately render the effects of external change on our inner consciousness. But, at the same time, the collapse of the Christian world view foreclosed retreat into a transcendental, ahistorical view of human events. Some combination of synthesis of horizontal, vertical, and circular perspectives had to be forged to render the concatenation of pressures shaping our situation. The great masterpieces of Proust, Mann, Joyce, Faulkner,

Broch, and Musil are the record of these attempts to achieve a synthesizing view of our culture.

For Butor, the writer's relationship to the literary tradition is one of both continuity and discontinuity: "an individual's work is a kind of knot produced within the cultural fabric at the heart of which the individual is not so much submerged, but rather *appears*. The individual is, from the beginning, a moment of this cultural fabric."[8] The writer must know what has been said as well as what remains to be said. He attempts to knit together existing discussions and extend them, developing new patterns and stitches in the process. Butor has described himself as a writer for whom "the great novels of the twentieth century have existed."[9] We have seen the general area of historical and cultural interest that Butor shares with the modernist masters; we need now to consider the ways he has gone beyond them.

One is immediately struck in surveying Butor's cultural inventory by its remarkable depth and breadth. He has unearthed a whole series of different levels beneath our present civilization: ancient Egypt, Greece, Rome, Byzantium, medieval Germany, the Renaissance, and the Age of Discovery, etc. Note also the geographical range: Europe, North Africa, and America. The net will be cast even wider, for his next major narrative *Boomerang*, scheduled for publication in 1978, will cover the southern hemisphere: Australia, New Zealand and the South Pacific. Butor's nearest rivals in historical and geographical ambition are Joyce and Pound, whose *Finnegans Wake* and *Cantos* include materials from an astonishing range of periods and areas. But merely to mention Joyce and Pound is also to set in relief a striking contrast between Butor and his predecessors. Greece, Rome, and the Renaissance come to us in *Finnegans Wake* and the *Cantos* in broken, often barely recognizable fragments, brilliant and beautiful, but dead. Butor, on the other hand, has painstakingly separated each layer, joined broken shards, and attempted to resurrect the essential genius of each of these cultures. Most of his narratives focus on a single area, penetrate to its heart, and seek to draw its past into a fruitful relationship with today. The modernist epics, on the other hand, tend to jumble the flotsam and jetsam of many places in a single, dazzling, but bewildering work.

These different approaches point up the fact that Butor imagines the past in a way fundamentally different from that of his modernist ancestors. The latter, try as they might to withdraw from history, were still profoundly marked by the nineteenth-century historical perspective. This model had, as we have seen, tragic implications for those artists and intellectuals who were attracted to the great civilizations of the past. The linear schema placed past and present at opposite ends of a long, straight line. The three modern novelists whom Butor studied most carefully—Proust, Joyce, and Faulkner—remained at least partially prisoners of the nineteenth-century historical perspective. For Joyce, the Homeric Golden Age occurred roughly 1200–900 B.C., some three thousand years distant from the Dublin day in 1904 described in *Ulysses*: such echoes and similarities as survived from that long-dead epoch must necessarily be fragmentary and ironic. Similarly, Faulkner's heroes find themselves isolated from the southern age of chivalry by an uncrossable gulf, a century of Civil War, Reconstruction, and racial bitterness. Proust does manage to capture the past, but this victory is only an individual's evanescent recovery of his personal experiences. There is no question of the revival of an entire historical epoch: the medieval world symbolized by Combray's church remains as remote as Joyce's Homeric Greece.

Butor, on the other hand, discovered on his first fateful voyage to the cradle of civilization that ancient Egypt was not irretrievably lost in the third millenium B.C. where the historians had placed it but is alive today. He found echoes of Egypt's sacred writings and architecture present in modern Judaism, Christianity, and Islam. More important, he found that the physical environment and many monuments were still there. Modern archeology had made it possible for the diligent student to penetrate into the world view in which the Pharaohs had lived. He found his own voyage into the Egyptian present-past enormously exciting and extremely fruitful for the shaping of his own attitudes.

His further voyages and studies only confirmed and generalized what he had discovered in Egypt. Bleston-Manchester revealed a whole series of temporal layers, forgotten and suppressed but still feebly present. *Réseau aérien* shows us that the remotest and least developed parts of the globe are no more than a day and a half from Paris; *Où*, reveals ancient Indian rituals, going back many centuries, a few hours outside modern Albuquerque. Butor had profited from a new perspective produced by the radical changes in communications and travel which, since World War II, have made the archeologists' and anthropologists' discoveries accessible and even visitable for all of us. Sharon Spencer describes the new approach to time:

> On earth today there exists virtually every historical period in the "progressive" history of man, ranging from the primitive culture of New Guinea to those societies whose technologies enable them to send men to walk on the moon. All these historical periods are *simultaneous*. What has changed is not their existence in time but our *awareness* of their

existence, an awareness that is made possible by the multiplication of perspectives achieved by cameras, radios, television and tape recorders. Every location is space; every *lieu* is infused with its own time, or simultaneity of times. In an important sense, time has lost its meaning apart from its aspect as a function of space as perceived by some individual from a changing point of view.[10]

Butor has replaced the two-dimensional historical model (a straight line, ascending or descending) with a three-dimensional one: the globe with different historical thicknesses at different points. Time becomes a function of space, and the magnificent machines we use to put ourselves in contact with other geographical areas can help put us in contact with other historical epochs. The past becomes *accessible* and *usable*. Once we abandon the old linear perspective we also begin to shed the prejudices inherent in it (anterior = inferior). Claude Lévi-Strauss has shown through anthropological research what Rousseau and Chateaubriand had intuited: the savage mind is not "primitive" or inferior; on the contrary, it is extremely sophisticated and, in certain areas, superior to the "civilized" mind. Once we shake off these prejudices we can begin to learn from people like the American Indian and the Egyptian who are at earlier stages of technological development.

Butor's attitudes toward the future contrast even more sharply with those of the modernists than do his attitudes towards the past. These earlier writers had also peered into what was to come, and their eyes were nearly blinded by the sight. D. H. Lawrence and Yeats prophesied a frightening Apocalypse. Writers like H. G. Wells, Aldous Huxley, and George Orwell who attempted detailed descriptions of the new society foresaw nightmarish anti-Utopias. Butor can face the future more cheerfully because of his confidence in our ability to use the past as we consciously shape our future. His different perspective also results from his ability to see the new technology, which the modernists feared as a force menacing humane culture, as a tool which can preserve and enrich the best of the past.

Butor's view of the past has caused him to develop his own distinctive way of presenting time in his narratives. His novels build on the modernists' experiments, using subjective temporal experiences, mythic parallels, the unities, and so forth to express the historical depths beneath Bleston, Paris, or Rome. His American texts, however, represent a significant development in his treatment of both time and space. For Butor, who has no European driver's license, although he does hold one valid in the United States, the characteristic mode of European travel is the train upon which Jacques Revel, Léon Delmont, and the young artist in *Portrait d'artiste en jeune singe* travel. In the United States, the great distances, the relative affluence, and the American's almost erotic love of the automobile make it and the airplane the characteristic modes of travel. Americans enjoy an extraordinary *mobility*, the capability of traveling great distances quickly and shorter ones according to one's own speed and interests. Since for Butor time and space are closely related, this greater spatial mobility also enables greater temporal movement.

Compare the spatial and temporal relationships in *La Modification* and his first American text, *Mobile*. Paris and Rome both have characteristic and quite deep "historical thicknesses." But if Jacques Revel wishes to travel between these two cities and the historical epochs buried within them, he can depart at either 8:10 A.M. or in the evening on the Rome express; in the former case the trip will take twenty-one hours and thirty-five minutes and in the latter eighteen hours and forty minutes. In both cases he will travel the same pre-ordained itinerary: Dijon, Bourg, Modano, and so forth. The Americans in *Mobile*, in contrast, jump on a jet and cross the entire continent in a few hours or use their autos to wander off the beaten path as they choose.

Beginning with *Mobile*, Butor has attempted to create a literary structure which would exploit the complex new spatial and temporal mobility of the "American age." *Mobile*'s continuing "national" texts represent virtually every period in America from before Columbus to the present, as the following list indicates:

Indian history, 800 B.C. through the nineteenth century
William Penn's treaty with the Delaware Indians, 1682
Salem witchcraft trial of Susanna Martin, 1692
Benjamin Franklin, "Information to Those Who Would Remove to America," 1782
Thomas Jefferson, "Notes on the State of Virginia," Letters, 1781–1806
Mormon history, early through mid-nineteenth century
Chicago and New York newspaper accounts of the Chicago Exposition, 1893
Andrew Carnegie, *The Gospel of Wealth*, 1900
Albert Hensley and John Rawe on the peyotl cult, 1910
Louis Sullivan, *The Autobiography of an Idea*, 1924
H. P. Lovecraft, "The Shadow Out of Time," "The Color Out of Space," "The Call of Cthulhu," 1927–1936
Brochures for Freedomland, Clifton's Cafeteria, Trappist Jelly, Chapel

Lake Indian Ceremonial and the Sears Roebuck catalog, 1960s.

Unrestrained by characters or plot, Butor roams widely and quickly through the states. Shifts between historical levels occur with equal rapidity. Texts from several different epochs stand side by side or in near proximity.

Jacques Revel, near the conclusion of his arduous year of excavation, experiences a climactic vision in which time is spatialized: the various historical levels buried within Bleston are juxtaposed, and Revel glimpses their relationship to each other and to the present. Butor attempts to generalize and extend throughout *Mobile* what is only a momentary occurrence in the novels. On virtually every page, past (in many cases, several pasts) and present stand together, revealing the presence and the influence of the former on the latter.

Butor's narratives differ significantly from those of his modernist predecessors, but what of his postmodernist contemporaries? Modernism, of course, survives in the work of writers as various and important As Heinrich Böll, Saul Bellow, Norman Mailer, and Gabriel García Marquez. Nonetheless, the appearance since 1950 of writers reacting against or attempting to go beyond modernism has caused critics to speak of a new, "postmodernist" fiction. The reaction against modernism takes several forms. "The literature of exhaustion" practiced by John Barth, Vladimir Nabokov, Jorge Luis Borges, and Samuel Beckett seeks to destroy the modernist art novel from within by parodying or "exhausting" its conventions. The new pop novel championed by Leslie Fiedler and practiced by Kurt Vonnegut, Thomas Berger, and Manuel Puig rejects modernist high-art pretensions out of hand and seeks to resuscitate the novel as a popular genre. Butor has little in common with either of these tendencies. He shares neither the despair nor the destructive tendencies of the literature of exhaustion, and, although popular forms like detective fiction interest him, he warns us against taking them as serious models for organizing our experience.

There is a third tendency, represented by the French *nouveau nouveau roman* and by American "surfiction," with which Butor has a certain affinity. These writers question not merely the modernist art novel but the notion of writing itself, and particularly its referential aspect. Butor's name has from the beginning of his career been associated with the *nouveau roman*, a group of experimental French novelists who won critical recognition in the early 1950s. Although never a formal movement or school, writers such as Butor, Alain Robbe-Grillet, Claude Simon, Claude Ollier, Robert Pinget, and Natalie Sarraute shared a common rejection of traditional, realist fiction and a commitment to the renovation of the French novel.

French experimental fiction reached a second stage in the early sixties. The emergence of Jean Ricardou and Phillipe Sollers, the appearance of the journal *Tel Quel*, and developments in the careers of Robbe-Grillet, Simon, and Ollier caused critics to speak of a *nouveau nouveau roman*. The point of attack increasingly became the idea of literature as it had developed in bourgeois culture. The representational, referential function of literature, no matter how experimental, was challenged. Against the instrumental, transparent use of language to describe a "real," extralinguistic world, the new new novelists proposed "scription," (*écriture*) which has no subject but itself, the free play of linguistic signs on a page. Jean Ricardou, Alain Robbe-Grillet, Claude Ollier, and Claude Simon produce texts by selecting a set of memories, quotations, allusions, or anagrams and then developing and combining these "generators". Ricardou has explained that he engendered the setting, characters, episodes, and descriptions of his *La Prise de Constantinople* (1965) out of nothing more than the elements of its title page. The adventure of writing, Ricardou maintained, had supplanted the writing of an adventure. Such activity might seem a recrudescence of late nineteenth-century art for art's sake aestheticism, but these new new novelists insist that their writing has serious social and political consequences. They argue that our notions of realistic, referential fiction grow out of and tend to support the dominant bourgeois ideology. Through their fictional experiments they hope to instruct us in the arbitrary character of language and of the ideology that we take for granted.

Butor has used generative techniques in his Don Juan poems, a series of texts printed on punched cards which can be shuffled into various combinations.[11] But Butor's narratives move in a direction different from that of the new new novelists. Butor repeatedly stated, beginning in the 1950s, his opposition to Robbe-Grillet's antirepresentational emphasis.[12] Robbe-Grillet returned the favor at the 1971 symposium on the new novel, noting Butor's absence from the assembly and calling attention to the fact that, despite formal similarities, Butor's purposes were different from his and those of other new novelists. Claude Ollier and Jean Ricardou, (who had included Butor in his critical discussions of the new novel) agreed.[13] Robbe-Grillet's film *Éden et après* (1971) and Butor's projected film *Intervalle* illustrate the contrasting directions their careers have taken: the former uses a complicated series of generators to turn in on itself and achieve aesthetic autonomy,[14] while Butor deliberately uses newspapers and recent events to make his work intersect with its surrounding social context.

American experimental fiction in the sixties underwent a transformation in many ways parallel to that of the French. The early and mid-sixties gave us the increasingly self-referential verbal play and literary parody of Nabokov and Barth, but a "radical disruption" occurred, according to Jerome Klinkowitz, in the publishing season of 1967–68.[15] Important experimental novels and story collections by Donald Barthelme, Ronald Sukenick, William Gass, Richard Brautigan, Steve Katz, and others all appeared within the same publishing year. (French fiction, according to Stephen Heath, took a crucial turn at virtually the same moment.)[16] Raymond Federman, a leading practitioner and theoretician of the new American fiction, describes the tendency represented by these new writers as "surfiction": "the primary purpose of fiction will be to unmask its own fictionality, to expose the metaphor of its own fraudulence and not pretend any longer to pass for reality, for truth, or for beauty. Consequently, fiction will no longer be regarded as a mirror of life, as a pseudorealistic document that informs us about life, nor will it be judged on the basis of its social, moral, psychological, metaphysical, commercial value, or whatever, but on the basis of what it is and what it does as an autonomous art form in its own right."[17] Donald Barthelme, Ronald Sukenick, and William Gass have made similar statements divorcing fiction from any representational responsibilities.

Federman, a teacher and scholar of French literature and an immigrant from France, is an important point of contact between the French and American schools. He explicitly identifies in his essays the general aims of the young Americans with those of Ricardou, Sollers, Beckett, Pinget, and Simon as well as with those of Argentina's Jorge Luis Borges and Italy's Italo Calvino. In a 1967 essay on *Mobile*, Federman confessed that Butor's text forced him to rethink his own ideas about the book.[18] His own first effort, *Double or Nothing* (1972), shares *Mobile*'s inventive typography and American setting. This book's verbal play, concrete poems, and personal tone tend, however, to turn it inward. Federman's subsequent fiction, both in English and in French, and his theoretical statements draw him closer to Ricardou and Sollers than to Butor. Butor's name is significantly missing from his list of surfictionists.

Mobile, one of Butor's most experimental works, bears the subtitle "a study for the *representation* of the United States." This admission of the book's representational intention, confirmed by its historical and sociological subject matter, seems to distance Butor from many important postmodernists. At the same time, we must also note that *Mobile* is a "*study* for the representation of the United States." There is in this subtitle, as well as in *Où*'s Sandia Mountain poems and in

Intervalle's *autocritique*, a recognition of the tentative, problematic character of any attempt to match words to external reality. *Mobile* is not realistic in any naive sense: it strenuously challenges our traditional notions about the way we represent the world to ourselves. The vigorously experimental character of Butor's work, never repeating the same form, each text trying to extend a bit further the power of language to describe our situation in history and society, reveals an anxious awareness of the limitations of language. It is in this recognition that Butor comes closest to the French and American surfictionists.

But this awareness takes Butor in another direction from these writers: he does not turn his back on society and history; instead he seeks to challenge and reform the ways we think and write about our experiences of time and space.[19] Other recent experimental novels, such as Julio Cortázar's *Rayuela*, Carlos Fuentes's *La Muerte de Artemio Cruz*, Uwe Johnson's *Jahrestage: Aus dem Leben von Gesine Cresspahl* and Thomas Pynchon's *Gravity's Rainbow*, share these concerns. But more than any other contemporary writer, Butor has maintained throughout his career a unique double commitment. He chooses, like the great novelists of the past, to focus on man in society and history; at the same time, he seeks to develop structures that will render this situation intelligible to a new age. Past and future. Janus.

Notes

Passages cited in the text have been taken, whenever possible, from the standard American translations with page numbers to these editions given in italics. Translations in all other cases are my own. The original French passages are given in the footnotes. Page numbers of the French editions are given in roman type.

Preface

1. *Répertoire III*, p. 403: La littérature est une transcription suspendue entre un passé à conserver et un avenir à préparer.

Introduction

1. "Le Nouveau Roman," mimeographed text of lecture distributed by Centre Européen Universitaire, Nancy, 1962-63, p. 3; Sartre était un philosophe et nous avions besoin d'une littérature sérieuse; la seule littérature qui pouvait nous importer était une littérature nous aidant à faire une carte ou un relevé de la réalité, une littérature nous permettant de voir et de comprendre ce qui subsistait au milieu de ces ruines, ce qui était solide.

2. *Répertoire III*, p. 64: voyager d'un lieu à un autre c'est voyager d'une épaisseur historique à une autre. See also *Répertoire II*, p. 96, and Jean Gaugeard, "Michel Butor: *Répertoire II*," *Les Lettres françaises*, no. 1022 (26 March, 1964), p. 4.

3. Quoted by Madeleine Chapsal, *Les Ecrivains en personne* (Paris: René Juillard, 1960), p. 67: Le rôle du romancier est d'amener une clarification, de permettre une prise de conscience des problèmes qui nous préoccupent. . . . la transformation du tissu mental dans lequel on vit, du milieu même où nous sommes plongés, du système où notre liberté prend ses références pour agir.

4. *Répertoire I*, p. 262: "Il faut changer la vie." Toute littérature qui ne nous aide pas dans ce dessein . . . est . . . inéluctablement condamnée. Butor is quoting Rimbaud, thus the internal quotes.

5. See "*Max Ernst* de Patrick Waldberg," *Critique* 15, no. 151 (1959), 1050-51, and *Répertoire II*, pp. 27-29.

6. "Michel Butor vous parle," *Université de Grenoble. Faculté des lettres et sciences humaines. Service de documentation. Bulletin d'information* (Oct.-Dec. 1968), p. 6: structures didactiques ou pédagogiques.

7. Henri Ronse, "Le Livre futur: un entretien avec Michel Butor," *Synthèses* 22, no. 248 (Jan. 1967), 106: Le livre est pour moi un moyen de connaître le monde et d'agir sur lui. . . . Se borner, comme font certains, à sa discipline, à son art, c'est refuser la réflexion, c'est choisir la stupidité et réduire bientôt cet "art" à n'être q'un artisanat. Pour moi, faire de la littérature, c'est s'occuper *ouvertement* du monde.

8. Jean Gaugeard, "Michel Butor: *Répertoire II*," *Les Lettres françaises*, no. 1022 (26 March, 1964), p. 4: l'histoire universelle.

9. *Répertoire I*, p. 15: archéologue mentale. See also *Travaux d'approche*, p. 179; *Répertoire II*, p. 92; and *Illustrations*, p. 22.

10. *Répertoire I*, p. 251: qui ignore tout de ce qui a mené à la situation dans laquelle il se trouve, ne peut pas parvenir à la conscience de soi. Il est en quelque sorte extérieur à lui-même, et sa conduite apparaît comme un inexorable destin.

11. Ronse, "Le Livre futur: un entretien avec Michel Butor," *Synthèses*, 22, no. 248 (Jan. 1967), 105: C'est pour cette raison que nous faisons de l'archéologie: pour savoir ce que nous sommes et que nous avions oublié, perdu tout en l'étant encore; pour retrouver ou découvrir la face inconnue de nous-mêmes.

12. *Répertoire III*, p. 22: Ce que nous cherchons dans l'archéologie, ce n'est pas tant notre passé que notre avenir, car ce qui fait naître une telle vocation c'est le fait que des oeuvres anciennes nous apparaissent comme des modèles précieux, riches d'un enseignement actuel; et il ne s'agit naturellement pas d'oeuvres isolées, la plupart du temps, mais de façons de vivre qui, par rapport à notre façon de vivre présente, ouvrent de nouvelles possibilités. L'émerveillement que nous ressentons dans les ruines de Rome ou de la Crète vient de ce qu'elles nous inspirent des changements pour nos maisons, nos villes et nos moeurs.

13. *The Hero with a Thousand Faces* (New York: Pantheon Books, 1949), p. 30.

14. Ibid., p. 30.

15. Ibid., p. 384.

16. Mircea Eliade, *The Quest: History and Meaning in Religion* (Chicago: Univ. of Chicago Press, 1969), p. 123.

17. Quoted by F. C. St. Aubyn, "Entretien avec Michel Butor," *French Review*, 36 (Oct. 1962), 19: tout cela ne prend son sens que dans le sens d'une analyse historique, que dans les relations de tout cela avec l'histoire universelle. *Matière de rêves* (1975) and *Second sous-sol, Matière de rêves 2* (1976) appear to be exceptions. Although these prose poems contain some historical themes, their reference is primarily personal.

18. Georges Charbonnier, *Entretiens avec Michel Butor*, p. 27: l'histoire entière soit devenue lumineuse, et que, par conséquent, nous sachions ce que nous voulons.

19. *Répertoire III*, p. 19: non le cercle fermé auquel on ne devrait rien pouvoir ajouter, mais la spirale qui nous invite à la poursuivre.

20. *Répertoire IV*, p. 24: nous fait remonter à la surface de l'autre côté de l'horizon normal, dénonce cette surface comme mensonge. Il s'agit d'une

ascension renversée, renversante, où le point d'arrivée situe le point de départ mais en lui faisant subir un retournement (c'est pourquoi ce point d'arrivée est si souvent conçu comme un centre), en le forçant à l'aveu.

21. St. Aubyn, "Entretien avec Michel Butor," pp. 20–21: Il faut qu'il y ait ce sacrifice humain à l'intérieur du roman. Dans la mesure où il accepte . . . d'être cette victime, dans cette mesure il réussit. Dans la mesure qu'il reconnaît que "cette musique future" lui est interdite mais que justement sa mort va la rendre possible pour d'autres, dans cette mesure-là il est entièrement pardonné.

22. Quoted by Georges Markow-Totevy, "Michel Butor," *Bucknell Review*, 10 (May 1962), 285.

23. *Intervalle*, p. 157: J'ai cru, oui, j'ai cru que le sort du monde dépendait, dans une mesure infime certes, mais dépendait de ce que j'écrivais, et lorsque je suis au fin fond du bagne de mon écriture, je l'avoue, je le crois toujours.

1. *Passage de Milan*

1. See Georges Charbonnier, *Entretiens avec Michel Butor*, p. 80.

2. "Symbolism in *Passage de Milan*," *French Review*, 42, no. 2 (Dec. 1968), 223-232.

3. Matins may be anticipated and read the day before. Ralon states that he has made a mistake by one day in reading this passage (162), thus the day may be Wednesday, Thursday, Friday or Saturday. The birthday party would surely not have been scheduled if there were classes the next day, nor would it have been probable that it be scheduled on Good Friday, so it is very likely that the book covers Holy Saturday evening and Easter morning.

4. See *Travaux d'approche*, p. 167.

5. *Le Génie du lieu*, p. 196: C'était une lueur sur mes origines et sur celle de la religion dans laquelle j'avais été élevé.

6. P. 284: beaux démons . . . profitent des fissures nocturnes.

7. P. 108: cette cérémonie si savante, qu'on dirait liée à des croyances primitives, très fondamentales et très oubliées.

8. P. 251: acteurs d'un drame liturgique.

9. Charbonnier, *Entretiens*, p. 53: C'est une fête de passage de la jeunesse à l'âge adulte. C'est en quelque sorte un équivalent, dans notre société, une ombre dans notre société, de fête d'initiation. Cette mise en relation de tous les éléments, de tous les individus vivant à l'intérieur du même immeuble va provoquer, non seulement la prise de conscience, pour chaque individu, des autres individus, mais aussi d'un certain nombre d'éléments communs qui traînent en quelque sorte dans leur conscience.

10. P. 235: divinité protectrice.

11. *Le Génie du lieu*, p. 110: seconde naissance.

12. Charbonnier, *Entretiens*, p. 54: une espèce de résonateur . . . une sorte de terme de référence, de point de comparaison.

13. *Le Génie du lieu*, p. 125: un espace où nous n'étions rien, comme le sol d'une planète autre . . . le roc usé par le vent, l'écorce sèche du globe.

14. *Travaux d'approche*, p. 74: prairie de la furie des dieux.

15. "Centre d'écoute, oeuvre où la musique joue un rôle déterminant," mimeo by the ORTF atelier pour la création radiophonique, Paris. 9 July, 1972, p. 14: l'aurore en Égypte n'a pas ces belles teintes vermeilles que l'on admire dans les Cyclades ou sur les côtes de Candie; le soleil éclate tout à coup au bord du ciel, précédé seulement d'une vague lueur blanche; quelquefois il semble avoir peine à soulever les longs plis d'un linceul grisâtre, et nous apparaît pâle et privé de rayons, comme l'Osiris souterrain. These lines are borrowed from Nerval's *Voyage en Orient*.

16. *Le Génie du lieu*, p. 132-33: Tout y apparaît éphémère, les hommes, certes, et tous les animaux domestiqués, mais aussi la configuration même du terrain.

17. Ibid., p. 187: conscience constante du caractère transitoire de l'individu, si différente de cette espèce d'oubli vis-à-vis de cette condition qu'il y a maintenant dans la plupart des pays de l'Europe occidentale.

18. Ibid., p. 134: l'organisation de leur société pour être stable devait elle-même intégrer un contraste, être fondée sur un équilibre de parties opposées.

19. P. 281: toute tête est un entrepôt, où dorment des statues de dieux et de démons de toute taille et tout âge, dont l'inventaire n'est jamais dressé.

20. P. 284: se rient de nous, cachés, se nourrissant de nos arrière-pensées.

21. *Le Génie du lieu*, p. 151: un fond noir et dangereux . . . hanté d'étranges lumières.

22. See ibid., p. 174.

23. See ibid., p. 208.

24. See ibid., p. 114; *Degrés*, pp. 84 and 141; *Où*, p. 111.

25. *Le Génie du lieu*, p. 192: des ensembles aussi énormes et prestigieux que l'Antiquité égyptienne ou l'Islam ne figurent dans leur représentation de l'univers que sous la forme d'appendices, de notes au bas des pages, de vignettes quasi humoristiques.

26. P. 76: leurs yeux s'ouvrir, l'envie du voyage se propager d'une tête à l'autre, comme un incendie d'arbre en arbre dans une forêt sèche, p. 87.

27. See *Le Génie du lieu*, pp. 199-200.

28. *Rabelais, ou c'était pour rire*, p. 90: modèle du langage futur, utopie.

29. P. 183: d'anciens pouvoirs, d'anciens désirs . . . d'anciennes craintes.

2. *L'Emploi du temps*

1. See also Butor's descriptions of dreary Northern England in *Illustrations II*, p. 266 ff. and "Centre d'écoute," p. 12.

2. *Passing Time*, pp. 35-36: Bleston n'est pas seule de son espèce . . . Manchester ou Leeds, Newcastle ou Sheffield, Liverpool . . . ou encore, sans doute, ces villes américaines, Pittsburgh ou Détroit, auraient eu sur moi une influence similaire, p. 38.

3. Quoted by Georges Charbonnier, *Entretiens avec Michel Butor*, p. 97: quelque chose de très important sur ce que sont les villes industrielles en général et par conséquent sur la civilisation occidentale actuelle.

4. P. *125*: Je trébuche au bord d'une faille au fond de laquelle le sol d'antan est resté nu, mesurant alors l'épaisseur de cette matière qu'il faut que je sonde et tamise, afin de retrouver des assises et des fondations, p. 120.

5. P. *4*: immense fossé, p. 10.

6. P. *195*: un fil d'Ariane, p. 187.

7. P. *104*: perpétuellement rendues brillantes par les baisers salés des lèvres bleues des eaux, p. 101.

8. P. *107*: cette Ariane, cette Phèdre . . . aux grands yeux, à la taille fine, aux seins offerts dans la grande ouverture de leurs corsages ajustés, aux seins semblables à des pêches sensibles, comme j'imagine ceux de Rose (maintenant n'importe quelle figure belle me ramène invinciblement vers la sienne), ceux de Rose sous son chandail bien fermé autour de son cou, pp. 103–4.

9. *Répertoire III*, p. 119: la *franchise* de l'Antiquité dans sa considération du corps humain.

10. Ibid., p. 120: la religion antique, bien loin d'interdire le regard, réussit à l'illuminer; la vision géniale d'Homère ou du sculpteur . . . transformait pour la société tout entière le spectacle de la nature.

11. *Le Génie du lieu*, p. 50: un contresens complet sur la Grèce—ces édifices insupportables dans leur prétentieuse vulgarité nous imposent le sentiment d'une profonde discontinuité historique.

12. P. *77*: père de tous les arts, p. 76.

13. P. *75*: Bleston, ville de tisserands et de forgerons, qu'as-tu fait de tes musiciens, p. 75.

14. See *Michel Butor ou le livre futur* (Paris: Gallimard, 1964), pp. 166–67.

15. P. *76*: à l'envers, p. 77.

16. Pp. *78–79*:

> Oui, la Rome des empereurs; elle avait pour correspondant, de l'autre côté, à gauche du choeur pour nous, mais à droite de ce Christ juge qui devait être représenté dans la grande verrière de l'abside, la Rome des papes, la capitale de l'Eglise.
>
> Il n'en reste rien?
>
> Il ne reste absolument rien des vitraux de l'autre côté.
>
> Les explications qu'il me donnait, loin de dissiper l'étrangeté, ne faisaient que la préciser et l'approfondir. Quelle ambiguité dans la disposition que ces verriers d'antan avaient donnée à leurs sujets, comme s'ils avaient voulu montrer, à travers l'illustration même de la lecture officielle de la Bible, qu'eux y découvraient autre chose. (pp. 78–79)

17. Enserré dans le labyrinthe des papes, p. 227. The phrase is omitted from the English translation.

18. *Répertoire II*, p. 175: la guerre entre deux systèmes de valeurs contradictoires, deux traditions, le "chrétien" et "l'antique."

19. P. *155*: deux grands hiéroglyphes qui inscrivent le meurtre au front de Bleston, au front de cette ville hantée de meurtre, p. 149.

20. P. *126*: un esprit d'une étonnante audace y dénaturait violemment les thèmes, les ornements, et les détails traditionnels, aboutissant ainsi à une oeuvre certes imparfaite, je dirais presque infirme, riche pourtant d'un pro-

fond rêve irréfutable, d'un sourd pouvoir germinateur, d'un pathétique appel vers des réussites plus libres et meilleures, p. 121.

21. See Georges Raillard, "L'Exemple," afterword to 10/18 edition of *L'Emploi du temps* published by Union Générale d'Editions (Paris: 1961), p. 501, n.

22. 'L'Art contemporain jugé par ses sources," *Les Lettres nouvelles* 9 (Feb. 1961), 135–36: Pensant les formes de son temps dans ce que je pourrais appeler un "espace architectural complet," c'est-à-dire reliant ses constructions à tous les aspects de la civilisation à l'intérieur de laquelle il les réalisait, Gaudi a pu les délivrer de leurs contradictions internes, et leur donner, par rapport à ces contradictions, une extraordinaire valeur novatrice dont nous recueillons aujourd'hui les fruits.

23. *P. 241*: cette façade en plein soleil, criant sa nouveauté, m'a fait presque oublier l'édifice déjà ancien que j'avais l'intention de visiter encore une fois . . . parce que je ne pouvais pas ne pas voir, au travers des hautes vitres blanches, cette énorme paroi de briques luisantes, cette preuve, hélas, de la vitalité de cette ville mauvaise, ce grand changement fait pour condamner tout vrai changement, p. 231.

24. Pp. *254–55*:
> intervenaient dans cette représentation de Rome, non seulement l'Athènes conquise, non seulement Pétra, Baalbeck, et Timgad, mais aussi cette ville de Bleston, cette ville de malédiction et d'oubli. l'ancienne ville de Bleston, Bellista, Belli Civitas, cette ville de mon malheur . . .

> et du même coup, cette ville, je l'ai vue elle-même dans une nouvelle lumière, comme si le mur que je longe depuis mon arrivée ici, par instants un peu moins opaque, soudainement s'amincissait, comme si une profondeur oubliée se déployait, de telle sorte que j'ai retrouvé le courage qui m'abandonnait, me sentant de nouveau capable, grâce à ces nouvelles lueurs, de m'en défier, de cette ville, de m'en protéger, de mieux lui résister. (pp. 244–45)

25. See *Illustrations II*, p. 234.

26. Charbonnier, *Entretiens*, p. 109: point d'interrogation.

27. *Répertoire III*, p. 19: Puisque l'ouvrage doit être indéfiniment continué par des lecteurs, en particulier ceux qui vont eux-mêmes en écrire d'autres plus ou moins clairement reliés à lui, il va bientôt se présenter de lui-même comme inachevé, non le cercle fermé auquel on ne devrait rien pouvoir ajouter, mais la spirale qui nous invite à la poursuivre.

28. *Répertoire II*, p. 240: Tout évangile qu'on prend pour l'évangile est un aprocryphe.

3. *La Modification*

1. *Répertoire III*, p. 122: non plus pour diviniser nos instincts mais pour les terrifier.

2. *P. 61*: dévergondage grandiose, p. 63.

3. *P. 243*: *pax romana* . . . une organisation impériale du monde autour d'une ville capitale, p. 231.

4.   P. *37*: où selon la tradition Jules César a vaincu les Gaulois, p. 42.

5.   P. *55*: le lac lamartinien, p. 57.

6.   P. *240*: foyer capital d'émerveillements et d'obscurités, p. 229.

7.   P. *206*: à l'intérieur de l'espace historique, p. 199.

8.   *Essais sur les essais*, p. 135: couvait en son coeur un paganisme philosophique.

9.   *Répertoire I*, p. 41: une structure religieuse qui s'inspire de plus en plus profondément du paganisme antique.

10.   See *Répertoire II*, p. 175: For a similar reading of Diderot, see *Répertoire IV*, p. 151.

11.   P. *52*: constant défi jeté par l'ancien Empire à l'actuelle Eglise, p. 55.

12.   P. *52*: base même de leur langage, p. 55.

13.   P. *46*: un chef-d'oeuvre auquel on a rajouté une tête parfaitement sotte, un bras, des pieds imbéciles qui lui enlèvent toute dignité (ne se trouvera-t-il donc pas à l'intérieur de cette cité depuis si longtemps pourrissante quelqu'un pour protester contre le scandale de ce désordre et de ce mensonge?), p. 50.

14.   *Le Génie du lieu*, p. 100: le centre du monde . . . pour justifier mythologiquement ce prodigieux privilège.

15.   Ibid., p. 65: le centre de son univers, l'"*omphalos*." On the night before departure, Delmont also listens to a recording of Monteverdi's "Orfeo" as he reads the *Aeneid*. Orpheus, who looks back and loses his lover, is perhaps an even more ironically appropriate presage of Delmont's own underground misadventure.

16.   P. *148*: hantés tous les deux par ces prophètes et ces sibylles, par ce Jugement absent, p. 144.

17.   *Le Génie du lieu*, p. 100: a été considéré pendant tout le Moyen Age comme la figure par excellence de ce qui dans la Rome impériale permettait la Rome chrétienne, comme le "prophète païen."

18.   *Studies in Iconology, Humanistic Themes in the Art of the Renaissance* (New York: Harper and Row, 1962), p. 177.

19.   C. P. Morey quoted by Panofsky in ibid., p. 177.

20.   Ibid., p. 229.

21.   There are other ironies in the Delmont-Julian parallel. Butor points out that Julian was famous for his chastity and that, through Montaigne's apologia, he became a symbol of French religious hypocrisy; see *Essais sur les essais*, pp. 132, 139.

22.   P. *199*; intoxiquée du rêve de l'Empire, p. 192.

23.   Jean Ralon also meets a serpent in his nightmares in *Passage de Milan* (219). Butor links the snake to the dispossessed but terrifying gods and goddesses at Delphi in *Génie du lieu* (78–79).

24.   *The New Novel* (New York: Farrar, Straus and Giroux, 1971), p. 220.

25.   Butor explained this structure in an interview "Michel Butor vous parle," *Université de Grenoble Faculté des Lettres et sciences humaine. Service de documentation. Bulletin d'information*, Oct.–Dec. 1968, pp. 4–5. See also . Jean Roudaut "Répétition et modification dans deux romans de Michel

Butor," *Saggi e ricerche di letteratura francese*, 3 (1967), 315–323 and Françoise VanRossum-Guyon, *Critique du roman, Essai sur La Modification de Michel Butor* (Paris: Gallimard, 1970), pp. 229–258.

26. P. *128*: Il ne faut plus penser à ce vieux voyage à Paris avec Cécile; il ne faut plus penser qu'à demain à Paris, p. 127.

27. Pp. *164–65*: aux démons non de vous seulement, mais de tous ceux de votre race, p. 159.

28.
Tout sera dit, tout sera fait, tout sera préparé. (chapter 5; 107)
Non, tout ne sera pas dit. (chapter 7; 167)

Vous vous posterez . . . pour guetter l'ouverture de ses persiennes. (chapter 2; 39)

Vous n'irez point guetter les volets de Cécile. (chapter 9; 227)

4. *Degrés*

1. P. *72*: nouvelle conscience, p. 82.

2. P. *104*: à te représenter ce que tu as été toi-même, donc d'où tu viens, donc dans quelle direction tu vas, quel est le vecteur de ton présent, p. 118.

3. Henri Ronse, "Michel Butor: 'Je ne suis pas un iconoclaste,' " *Les Lettres françaises*, no. 1178 (April 1967), 6: nous naissons à l'intérieur des livres . . . de telle sorte que l'on peut dire de chacun d'entre nous que nous avons été *lus* avant de parler.

4. Hubert Juin, "Une Heure de cours de histoire, une interview de Michel Butor," *Les Lettres françaises*, no. 807 (14 Jan. 1960), 5: espace mental.

5. P. *102*: ces dificultés qui se dévoilent à moi maintenant, à chaque page, de plus en plus vertigineuses, et qui sont liées aux contradictions mêmes de cette société que nos constituons, éleves et professeurs, contradictions que je cherche par ce texte à te présenter pour qu'en toi quelques-unes au moins se résolvent, p. 116.

6. "Influences de formes musicales sur quelques oeuvres," *Musique en jeu*, no. 4 (1971), 67: *Degrés* est fondé sur les échos qui existent dans le temps . . . c'est une étude sur les résonances.

7. Pp. *58, 103, 225, 285*: la découverte et la conquête de l'Amérique, pp. 66, 117, 253, 318.

8. P. *58*: cette multiplication par deux soudainement des dimensions de l'univers, p. 66.

9. Pp. *10*, 12-13. Butor makes a similar comparison elsewhere when he describes archeologists as "Christophe Colomb du temps" discovering whole new worlds in the past, *Répertoire III*, p. 22.

10. P. *29*: c'est ce changement du visage du monde qui a nécessité une réforme de l'enseignement, p. 34.

11. P. *113*: liaison entre la mise en question de la tradition universitaire par les humanistes à propos des textes littéraires, scientifiques ou philosophiques de l'antiquité, et la mise en question de la tradition ecclésiastique par Luther à propos des textes sacrés, p. 130.

12. Maria Craipeau, "Entretien avec Michel Butor," *France-Observateur*, no. 506 (14 Jan. 1960), 19: montrer notre culture. . . . on se rend compte

combien elles [les connaissances à notre portée] sont énormes. Tant de choses, tant de gâchis. Ces connaissances qu'on sert aux élèves sans aucune corrélation, sans qu'ils soient en mesure de comprendre, d'assimiler."

13.

la conquête de l'Amérique . . . l'organisation du travail forcé dans les mines, le début de la traite des noirs, l'afflux d'or en Espagne, le développement des banques dans toute l'Europe (16)

l'essor du capitalisme, le développement des chemins de fer et des villes noires (53)

la transformation des sociétés européenes après la découverte de l'Amérique, de l'élévation du coût de la vie . . . l'essor prodigieux des banquiers, Fugger, Médicis, l'abaissement du niveau de vie dans les classes pauvres (181)

le mercantilisme européen . . . l'Europe exploite le monde (231)

14.   *Répertoire I*, p. 245: Il y a certes dans cette thèse une grande vérité, qui apparaît immédiatement dès que l'on donne au mot usure son équivalent moderne, le capitalisme.

15.   P. *98*:

ces hommes dont l'agitation était semblable à celle intérieure à une montagne volcanique,

dont le travail haineux, dont la fureur garottée, dont la fermentation constamment contenue par des polices et des clergés que l'image ne montrait pas, faisait vomir par le cratère un peu d'argent transporté à grand mal, à grandes pertes, à grande cruauté, jusqu'aux ports, puis, á travers la mer, jusqu'á l'Espagne,

avant de fendiller tout ce nouvel empire, mûrissant et cuisant peu à peu une énorme vengeance sournoise, dont les fumées ne se développeraient que beaucoup plus tard, n'avaient pas terminé sans doute même aujourd'hui leur expansion. (112).

16.   Pp. *48–49*:

notre représentation habituelle de ce qui se passe dans le monde contemporain, et de l'histoire universelle, est constamment fausée par la prééminence dans nos esprits de la projection cylindrique, dite projection de Mercator, employée dans presque tous les planisphères, ceux que l'on trouve dans les agences des compagnies de navigation, aussi bien que dans les écoles ou les dictionnaires, et qui a la particularité de majorer considérablement les surfaces des pays des zones tempérées et polaires au détriment de ceux de la zone équatoriale,

si bien qu'il nous faut souvent faire un effort considérable pour apprécier les véritables relations de masses qui existent entre des pays comme la France et l'Angleterre, par exemple, et d'autre part l'Inde ou la Chine. (56)

17.   *Le Genie du lieu*, p. 192: schéma qui se donne comme suffisant, comme devant permettre toutes les explications sans qu'il soit besoin de faire intervenir ces autres peuples, ces autres civilisations bizarres, curieuses, exotiques, amusantes, mais auxquelles un esprit sérieux, rassis, un monsieur qui s'occupe d'affaires ou de politique considère qu'il ne saurait sans ridicule

accorder une attention véritable, de telle sorte que des ensembles aussi énormes et prestigieux que l'Antiquité égyptienne ou l'Islam ne figurent dans leur représentation de l'univers que sous la forme d'appendices, de notes au bas des pages, de vignettes quasi humoristiques.

18. Ibid., p. 162: Le ressentiment sourd contre l'Europe . . . l'envie, le malaise, le besoin douloureux et muet d'une réorganisation de toute la figure du monde.

19. P. *79*: cette exclusivité de la civilisation qu'elle continue à s'arroger en dépit de toutes les preuves qu'elle a elle-même déterrées, et qu'elle continue elle-même à chercher et produire, nourrissant cette contradiction, cette grande fissure, ce grande mensonge qui la mine, p. 91.

20. P. *42*: l'homme est un microcosme, p. 49.

21. P. *95*: éducation raisonnable, raisonnable pour un géant, cela va sans dire, p. 109.

22. F. C. St. Aubyn, "Entretien avec Michel Butor," *French Review* 36, (Oct. 1962), 20: cette catastrophe que le livre raconte et produit en même temps.

23. P. *58*: Il existait peut-être, à la fin du XVe siècle, deux frères ou deux cousins Fage, qui se sont dit adieu au moment même où les navires de Colomb quittèrent pour la première fois Cadix à la recherche du Catai, et ne se sont jamais revus, dont les descendants n'ont plus jamais eu de rapports jusqu'au jour où deux d'entre aux ayant convergé vers Paris, pp. 66–67.

24. P. *79*: un noir qui vient des Caraïbes, et toute cette leçon sur l'Amérique, sur le désir de l'Amérique, sur le malheur de l'Amérique, la vengeance d l'Amérique, son énigme, le touche particulièrement, p. 90.

25. P. *98*: constamment contenue par des polices et des clergés, p. 112.

26. P. *101*: le contraire de liens, des liens négatifs, p. 115.

27. P. *102*: liées aux contradictions mêmes de cette société que nous constituons, élèves et professeurs, p. 116.

28. Unnumbered, last page: la réforme de l'enseignement.

29. P. *347*: une ruine . . . vestige d'une conscience et d'une musique future, p. 385.

30. St. Aubyn, "Entretien avec Butor," pp. 20–21. See Introduction, note 22 above.

31. *Essais sur les essais*, p. 214: un ami futur qui remplira la place prête pour lui.

32. P. *347*: tour d'où l'on devait voir l'Amérique, p. 385.

33. *The Poetics of Quotation in the European Novel*, trans. Theodore and Yetta Ziolkowski (Princeton, New Jersey: Princeton Univ. Press, 1968), pp. 19–20.

34. Anne Fabre-Luce, "Du Mouvement en littérature: Entretien avec Michel Butor," *Cahiers du XXe Siècle*, no. 1 (1973), 9: L'auteur est dans la salle parmi ses lecteurs. Le texte ne va pas de l'auteur-professeur au lecteur-auditeur-élève, il naît du dialogue des élèves entre eux. L'auteur est l'instrument de la stabilisation transformatrice d'un récit qui est déjà là.

5. *Description de San Marco* and
Portrait d'artiste en jeune singe

1.   *Le Génie du lieu*, pp. 51–52: Salonique, à mi-chemin entre Athènes et Constantinople . . . est par excellence le lieu où éprouver cette évidence prodigieusement méconnue, que de l'éclatante civilisation hellénique jusqu'à notre temps il n'y a pas seulement ce chemin qui passe par Rome et la Renaissance italienne, mais aussi, l'entrecoupant d'ailleurs plus souvent qu'on ne l'imagine, celui que jalonnent les monuments de l'empire et l'Eglise d'Orient.

2.   *Degrés*, p. *32*: poignante splendeur byzantine, p. 38. See also *Rabelais, ou c'était pour rire*, p. 56.

3.   *Répertoire II*, p. 278: où se réunissent l'Orient et l'Occident.

4.   Pp. 14-15: repérée sans doute par Néron pour couronner son arc de triomphe, transportée par Constantin dans sa nouvelle Rome où elle couronnait l'hippodrome, et raflée en dernier lieu par Napoléon pour l'arc de triomphe du Carrousel où elle resta jusqu'à ce que le congrès de Vienne en eût ordonné la restitution.

5.   Pp. 20–21: il était impossible de laisser dire aux visiteurs que toute la splendeur de Saint-Marc était ce qui venait de la grande ville impériale unique source. Il fallait donc enserrer tout cela dans un tissu nouveau.

6.   P. 24: la basilique est si puissante qu'elle absorbe en son mur le corps même de ses ennemis.

7.   Pp. 69–70: violation flagrante et délibérée de la tradition byzantine, soulignant en particulier tout ce qu'il peut y avoir de non byzantin dans les mosaïques de cette région.

8.   P. 26: une architecture d'images . . . une architecture de textes.

9.   P. 32: la bible de Saint-Marc va nous donner une adaptation vénitienne du catholicisme, souvent fort éloignée de la tradition romaine.

10.   P. 31: " . . . Alors Yahvé Dieu modela l'homme avec la glaise du sol," version particulièrement intéressante pour Venise, la naissance de l'homme étant liée à la séparation de la glaise et des eaux, à la constitution de l'archipel vénitien. La lagune reproduit les origines de l'humanité, et ses habitants acquièrent par là même une autorité, un droit sur autrui.

11.   P. 89: Au-dessus de la grande tribune, conclusion de tout cela, le Jugement universel, paradis au sommet, et, par la grande baie, ce qui devrait être une figure de la Jérusalem céleste, Venise, le ciel de Venise.

12.   See "Marges pour l'Apocalypse" in *La Gloire de Dürer* (Paris: Klincksiek, 1974), p. 216 and "A Paris," *L'Oeil français*, no. 54 (June 1959), p. 38.

13.   See *Intervalle*, p. 54.

14.   voyage aussi dans le temps: le XVIIIe siècle s'achève à peine en quelques îlots de cette région, crépuscule du Saint Empire.

15.   "Butor s'explique", *Le Monde*, no. 6902 (22 March 1967), p. 5: "faire une composition dans le style allemand du dix-huitième siècle avec tout ce qui y reste de médiéval et exprimer ainsi notre relation profonde au Moyen Age. See also Henri Ronse, "Michel Butor: 'Je ne suis pas iconoclaste'," *Les Lettres françaises*, no. 1178 (13 April 1967), p. 6, and Claudio Barbati,

"Incontro con Michel Butor, autore della 'Modificazione'; Un Ingegnere alla ricerca della realtà perduta," *La Fiera letteraria*, 40, no. 43 (3 Nov. 1966), 7.

16. P. 32: superlivre.

17. "Butor s'explique," p. 5: la dichotomie chrétienne, matière et esprit, qui aboutit au dualisme cartesien.

18. *Répertoire I*, p. 15: archéologue mentale.

19. See "Michel Butor: 'Je ne suis pas iconoclaste'," p. 1.

20. P. 105: une bulle de temps passé.

21. P. 21: cette flaque d'Asie.

22. P. 105: je savais que le silence de la cellule était comme un fragile pont bâti sur un gouffre de hurlement.

23. P. 113: la demeure philosophale.

24. Pp. 207–09:

> ô beauté, protège-moi, beauté! . . .
> ô clarté, protège-moi! . . .
> contre l'horreur qui rôde protège-moi! . . .
> contre ces grondements, contre ces grognements,
> contre ces craquements, contre ces
> ronflements, contre ces ricanements. . . .

25. Jennifer Walters, "Literary Alchemy," *Diacritics*, 2, no. 1 (Winter 1971), 8; Thomas O'Donnell, "Polemics," *Diacritics*, 2, no. 2 (Summer 1972), 52–56.

6. *Mobile*

1. See "Leonce Peillard s'entretient avec Michel Butor," Michel Butor repond au questionnaire Marcel Proust *Livres de France*, no. 6 (June-July 1963), p. 9.

2. P. *347*: tour d'où l'on devait voir l'Amérique, p. 385.

3. Georges Charbonnier, *Entretiens avec Michel Butor*, p. 233: un voyage à l'intérieur de sa propre histoire, . . . à l'intérieur de ses propres contradictions.

4. Jack Kolbert, "An Interview with Michel Butor," *American Society of Legion of Honor Magazine*, 45, no. 2 (1974), 91. See also George Raillard, *Butor* (Paris: Gallimard, 1968), pp. 164–65.

5. "Les Etats-Unis et mon livre *Mobile*," recorded interview with Hughes Dasalle. *Collection Français de Notre Temps*, no. 57, 1965: j'ai fait de l'archéologie sur ce pays tout à fait vivant.

6. Charbonnier, *Entretiens*, p. 231: avec leurs problèmes et leurs contradictions européennes qui ont trouvé un espace dans lequel, ces contradictions ont en quelque sorte fleuri. . . . Le problème des Etats-Unis c'est le problème de ce que devient la civilisation européenne lorsqu'elle arrive dans un paysage qui lui permet de se développer à plus grande échelle.

7. See F. C. St. Aubyn, "A propos de *Mobile*: Deuxième entretien avec Michel Butor," *French Review*, 38 (Feb. 1965), 432, 435-36.

8. à travers un continent, à travers des siècles.

9. P. *125: La pratique religieuse la plus importante des Européens d'Amérique est le pèlerinage à la ville sacrée de Washington, où se trouvent les principaux temples et les organes essentiels du gouvernement.* . . . *Le territoire de cette ville, quasi rectangulaire (on sait quelle valeur fondamentale les Européens d'Amérique ont accordée à l'angle droit), est enclavé dans l'Etat de Maryland, mais il n'en fait point partie. C'est un espace à part,* p. 131.

10. P. *131: La religion de Washington est la seule à être pratiquée par tous les Européens d'Amérique,* p. 137. Elsewhere Butor irreverently subverts this American dogma by highlighting key passages in Jefferson's writings which reveal his racism (*115, 265*; 120, 277) and by juxtaposing Ben Franklin's pronouncements on American egalitarianism with Andrew Carnegie's "Gospel" justifying a wealthy American aristocracy (*232,* 243).

11. *Répertoire II,* p. *175:* la guerre entre deux systèmes de valeurs contradictoires, deux traditions, le "chretien" et l' "antique."

12. Ibid., p. 171: Le rêve de devenir Sauvage, c'est tout d'abord l'espoir d'une libération érotique, et c'est pourquoi la caractéristique décisive de "l'état de nature," c'est la nudité.

13. Ibid., p. 172: A la nudité 'fière,' harmonie avec la nature intérieure, l'instinct, est étroitement liée la vie dans la forêt, harmonie avec la nature extérieure, proximité de celle-ci, liaison avec les animaux, les plantes, le spectacle de la nature en général.

14. P. *36: Méfiez vous de ce continent,* p. 37. See also *Histoire Extraordinaire,* pp. *132,* 196.

15. "Oedipus Americanus," preface to William Styron, *La Proie des flammes* (Paris: Gallimard, 1962), p. xx: oubli historique.

16.

Les Européens ont épucé la prairie de ses bisons et de ses Indiens. (60)

Les Européens ont tracé sur la prairie de grandes lignes perpendiculaires. (60)

Les Européens ont recouvert la prairie d'une mince pellicule comme une couche de peinture, sur laquelle les réserves font des accrocs. (61)

Et, dans la terreur, les Européens exilés ont commencé d'attendre leur récolte. (63)

17. P. *103: expression, visage, langage de ce continent scandaleux,* p. 107.

18. P. 27: Comme il est naturel que ce soit en ce monument qu'ait choisi de se faire inhumer l'Inca Garcilaso de la Vega, bâtard d'un capitaine conquérant et d'une princesse de Cuzco, demeurant si profondément indien malgré la sincérité de son christianisme; comme il est naturel que ce soit en cette cité, admirable figure de la sourde persistance agissante d'une civilisation, qu'il ait décidé de se fixer pour nous transcrire en ce chef-d'oeuvre que sont ses *Commentaires royaux,* les récits qu'il avait entendu raconter dans son enfance.

19. P. *137: prodigieux accumulateurs* . . . *se diffusent des vagues des rêves,* p. 143.

20. Pp. *219-20: Toutes les parcelles de ce sol sont sacrées* . . . *La nuit,*

lorsque tout bruit aura cessé dans les rues de vos villages, et que vous les croirez désertes, elles grouilleront de la foule de ceux qui ont vécu là autrefois, fidèles à ce sublime lieu. Jamais l'homme blanc n'y sera seul, p. 230.

21. P. *104*: *ils nous ont servi à nous masquer ces yeux indiens, le regard indien, le scandale indien. Entre cette terre qui nous disait: non, vous n'êtes pas en Europe, et nous qui voulions que ce fût l'Europe, nous avons étendu cet écran noir*, p. 109.

22. P. *108*: *une sorte de connivence*, p. 112.

23. P. *145*: *Je sens dans son odeur toute l'odeur des bois, des marais et du fleuve. Alors, je ne puis même plus retenir les draps sur ma poitrine; malgré tous mes efforts je sais que mes doigts se desserrent. Son visage est juste au-dessus du mien. Dehors s'ouvrent les fleurs du magnolia. Il pose sa main sur ma chemise; il y fait une grande tache brûlante. Mon coeur bat dans ma poitrine à coups tellement précipités. Il ouvre son pantalon*, p. 151.

24. P. *253*: *la puissance qui croît dans leurs ténèbres*, p. 264.

25. P. *269*: *c'est votre civilisation qu'ils menacent, ils ne laisseraient presque rien subsister de votre "american way of life!"* p. 280.

26. Charbonnier, *Entretiens*, p. 173: *couleur quasi sacrée aux Etats-Unis.*

27. P. *303*: *rafraîchissantes ténèbres*, p. 316.

28. P. *318*: *La nuit aux aurores boréales.* . . . *La nuit claire pleine d'étoiles*, p. 332.

29. See St. Aubyn, "A propos de *Mobile*," p. 427.

30. Ibid., p. 439: espoir utopique . . . d'un monde veritablement nouveau.

31.
Comme nous t'attendons,
Amérique!
Comme nous attendons ton retournement! (329)
Aide-nous nuit!
O complicité!
O sourde Amérique la nuit!
Terra incognita! (331)

7.   *6.810.000 litres d'eau par seconde*

1. *Répertoire II*, p. 182: le côté spectaculaire de la nature américaine . . . le coeur même, le foyer de cette nature différente.

2. P. *5*: *c'est moins une rivière qu'une mer impétueuse dont les cent mille torrents se pressent à la bouche béante d'un gouffre*, p. 13.

3. P. *134*: l'oracle, lares du continent, p. 143.

4. P. *44*: fontaine de Jouvence, p. 51. See also *Répertoire II*, p. 179–80.

5. P. *217*: un véhicule en forme de cercueil pour forcer la port des morts, p. 226.

6. Pp. *126–28*: Un éclair, à travers toutes les vitres ruisselantes, jette sa lueur sur les draps, dans la nuit noire, dans la pluie noire; sang; pluie de sang, pluie de sang noire, pluie de vieux sang noire dans la nuit, le sang de massacrés revenant mugissant dans la nuit noire, pp. 135–36.

7. P. *200*: eaux de l'oubli, p. 209.

8. P. *205*: cataracte de larmes, p. 213.

9. P. *151*: Pour tant de couples amoureux maintenant, it est temps d'affronter de nouveau la route. . . . Ceux qui voulaient rester plusieurs jours encore ici, mais qui ne savent plus, p. 161.

10. Pp. *62–64*: Ils ne sentent pas. . . . Ils ne savent pas. Mais tu sais sentir. . . . Mais tu sais flairer. Mais tu sais fouiller. . . . Ils ne savent plus se regarder. Ne savent plus nous regarder. . . . Il y a quelque chose en eux qui regarde encore. Il y a quelque chose en eux qui est étouffée. . . . Ils nous ont vus, mais ils nous auront évités. Nous allons troubler leur première nuit, p. 69–71.

11. P. *50*: Tes mains couvertes de terre que tu lavais pour me caresser, mais qui sentaient le savon et la terre avec l'odeur des roses au-dessus du fumier et tes ongles encore tout encadrés de terre comme de jeunes pousses, p. 57.

12. Georges Charbonnier, *Entretiens avec Michel Butor*, p. 229: dans la conscience américaine il y a là une espèce de chute. . . . Il y a le Niagara qui tombe brusquement et après cette chute commence l'histoire des Etats-Unis comme pays occidental.

13. *Règpertoire II*, p. 300: la mentalité américaine s'inscrit dans les millions d'objets manufacturés.

14. P. *6*: *chaos des ondes*, p. 14.

15. Charbonnier, *Entretiens*, p. 179: traitement homéopathique.

16. *Histoire Extraordinaire*, pp. *132–33*:
Ainsi, c'est parce que le puritain ne parvient pas à éteindre en lui les appels de ce mal, de cet homme sauvage, de cette sensualité et de cette invention, qu'il clame si fort ses réussites dans le domaine de la production commerciale, et qu'il étale tant son argent. L'industrie dont le mérite immense est qu'elle permet la modernité, se corrompt elle aussi, devient malade. Ce fard si précieux devient lèpre. Ce qui devait surpasser la nature ne cherche plus qu'à l'effacer, qu'à la défigurer. (196)

17. *Répertoire II*, p. 182: Il n'évoque nullement la stérilité, le Sahara; au contraire, ce désert est caractérisé par le splendeur de sa flore . . . un lieu que la société humaine a laissé intact.

18. *Réalités*, no. 197, p. 76; *Illustrations*, pp. 94–104:
Quand les pionniers allant vers l'Ouest et l'or, après des semaines et des semaines dans les plaines et la prairie, apercevaient la grande muraille de rocs, de pics et de forêts, ils savaient qu'au-delà commençaient les déserts, l'immensité menaçante, le pays de l'étonnement, et qu'il faudrait y résister, y subsister pendant des semaines et semaines avant d'atteindre l'autre grande chaine, et descendre enfin vers le Pacifique.
Quand l'automobiliste, aujourd'hui, après des heures, des heures, des jours de route droite dans l'interminable ferme du Middle-West, est salué par le monde sauvage, à l'intérieur duquel il lui faudra se faufiler, minuscule et seul, avec précautions, c'est comme une gigantesque respiration qui le saisit, un vent venu du fond des âges, lui, Américain, citoyen d'une nation si rapidement vieillie, se retrouve neuf, au seuil du plus inquiétant des paradis.

Quand l'avion quitte le quadrillage vert dont la régularité s'accentuait de l'Indiana à l'Illinois, de l'Iowa au Nebraska, pour franchir, dans l'Etat de Colorado, les monts outremer sommés de nacre, et baigner dans la surprenante couleur du sol qui change constamment au-dessous de lui, le jeune voyageur est pris d'un vertige tout autre: en quelques instants, lui semble-t-il, le monde déploie à ses yeux plus de secrets que pendant des années d'études autrefois.

19. *Illustrations*, p. 100: Votre respiration devient un tel tumulte que vous avez envie de la retenir, mais vous poussez un cri qui s'éteint.

20. Ibid., p. 94: le bruit, le grondement répercuté par les parois taillées.

21. *Mobile*, p. *151: Je rêve des bisons, de troupeaux de chevaux, des Indiens de la prairie, des Saints du Dernier Jour et de leur marche à travers les Etats, des nouvelles terres*, p. 157. See also *Rèseau aérien*, p. 38.

8. *Où, Le Génie du lieu, 2*

1. "Comment se sont écrits certains de mes livres," *Nouveau Roman: hier, aujourd'hui*, (Paris: Union Générale d'Editions, 1972), 2: 253: deux pôles.

2. *Où,* p. 190 (2 Nephi 5: 21-22): Et il fit venir sur eux une malédiction . . . . alors, comme ils étaient blancs, beaux et séduisants à l'excès, pour qu'ils pussent devenir une tentation pour mon peuple, le Seigneur Dieu leur fit venir une peau de noirceur. . . . je les rendrai haïssable aux autres peuples.

3. Ibid. p. 160 (Jacob 2: 24): une abomination pour le Seigneur.

4. P. 177: la perle de grand prix.

5. P. 266: le lieu où tout a commencé.

6. "Introduction to Zuni Ceremonialism," *Forty-Seventh Annual Report of the Bureau of American Ethnology* (Washington D.C.: U.S. Government Printing Office, 1932), p. 486.

7. P. 367: proclame la stabilité de l'espace.

8. P. 376: c'est comme si le soleil était mort et ne dût jamais revenir.

9. For two very worthwhile discussions of these poems and of *Où* generally see Leon S. Roudiez *French Fiction Today* (New Brunswick, N.J.: Rutgers Univ. Press, 1972), pp. 310–14 and Donald B. Rice, "The Exploration of Space in Butor's *Où*," in George Stambolian, ed., *Twentieth Century French Literature: Essays for Germaine Brée* (New Brunswick, N.J.: Rutgers Univ. Press, 1975), pp. 198–222.

10. See *Répertoire III*, pp. 164–67.

11. P. 389: tous les mots précédents s'écroulent en poussière c'est comme un cri de plus en plus intense . . . je m'efforce encore une fois de tendre mon filet miniscule sur cette proie énorme.

12. *Répertoire IV*, p. 24: nous fait remonter à la surface de l'autre côté de l'horizon normal, dénonce cette surface comme mensonge.

13. P. 392: Mais je reviendrai. C'est pour te faire boire que je reviendrai. Tous les voyages que je fais dessinent ta palpitation. Et c'est pour toi, pour toi, que je respire ici.

9. *Intervalle*

1. P. 93: Venise du centre.

2. P. 69: ce pays brumeux.

3. P. 104: l'hiver vénitien, la brume.

4. *Oeuvres complètes* (Paris: Gallimard, 1956), vol. 2.

5. P. 161: *Pendant que nous rasions la côte . . . j'avais aperçu un petit monument, vaguement découpé sur l'azur du ciel, et qui, du haut d'un rocher, semblait la statue encore debout de quelque divinité protectrice . . . Mais, en approchant davantage, nous avons distingué clairement l'objet qui signalait cette côte à l'attention des voyageurs. C'était un gibet.*

6. P. 161–62: *L'Egypte est un vaste tombeau; c'est l'impression qu'elle m'a faite en abordant sur cette plage d'Alexandrie, qui, avec ses ruines et ses monticules, offre aux yeux des tombeaux épars sur une terre de cendres. Des ombres drapées de linceuls bleauâtres circulent parmi ces débris.*

7. P. 86: l'île de Vénus n'était point fichée d'un gibet.

8. P. 86: est-il vraiment aujourd'hui une seule région où l'ombre, la puanteur de quelque croix n'interdise pas le regard?

9. P. 133: mettant ainsi l'information en perspective.

10. *Répertoire IV*, p. 13: Voyage, mot mille fois répété dans nos rues, dans la publicité, il est la séduction même. Il nous entraîne dans l'agence.

11. Ibid., p. 17: c'est la plage alors, ou le champ de ski. Quittez vos soucis! Evadez-vous!

12. Ibid., p. 19: le voyage au . . . site oraculaire; on y apporte sa question, on en attend une réponse, guérison du corps ou de l'âme. Le lieu saint se détache au milieu de régions profanes; il est la lucarne sur le paradis. Puis le pèlerinage devient voyage aux lieux qui parlent, qui nous parlent de notre historie et de nous-mêmes.

13. Ibid., p. 26: Le pèlerinage de Chateaubriand est un voyage dans l'histoire, celui de Gérard dans le mensonge de l'histoire.

14. *Répertoire IV*, p. 11: L'échappée qu'elle permet au quotidien blessant, pressant, haineux, obscur, fait de la lecture une cérémonie de purification. . . . L'ailleurs que nous donne le livre nous apparaît, de par la traversée de la page, comme pénétré de blancheur, baptisé. Parfois le refus du monde tel qu'il est, le découragement devant les difficultés de sa transformation, deviennent si forts que le lecteur préfère rester dans le suspens de cette blancheur, enfin tranquille.

15. P. 96: soubresauts du texte, c'est là mon vrai roman.

16. P. 90: soldats ni de religieuses, ni de salle d'attente à Lyon-Perrache. . . . aura en quelque manière contribué à l'abolition de l'horrible aujourd'hui.

17. "Michel Butor en 40 Questions," *La Galérie*, no. 106 (July 1971), 64. Je prépare une autre civilsation, une vie autre.

18. See *Histoire Extraordinaire*, pp. *64–65*, 99–102 and *L'Arc*, no. 39, p. 86.

19. The poem appeared in *Topique*, nos. 4–5 (1970), pp. 99–101. The essay is included in *Répertoire IV*.

20. *Répertoire III*, p. 151: l'instauration du christianisme avec sa censure furieuse sur la sexualité a été un moyen de conserver la réalité de l'esclavage

tout en en supprimant le nom. See also Pierre Hahn, "Onze écrivains et éditeurs nous disent ce qu'ils pensent de la littérature érotique," *Magazine littéraire*, no. 13 (Dec. 1967), p. 20.

21. *Dialogues avec 33 variations de Ludwig van Beethoven sur une valse de Diabelli*, p. 107: la milice infatigable des ouvriers . . . et la phalange des travailleurs, des penseurs, abaissera un jour la puissance aveugle des rois, des ministres despotiques d'Adonaï.

22. *Répertoire IV*, p. 194: déploie à nos yeux, dans ses divagations cosmogoniques, un monde immense et burlesque, sans se soucier de preuves ni de vraisemblance.

23. "Vivre avec Fourier," *Critique*, no. 281 (Oct. 1970), p. 792.

24. *Répertoire IV*, p. 434: Le livre est tellement central dans notre civilisation que si nous ne pouvons les changer que corrélativement, il est sans doute le point d'attaque par excellence. . . . Ecrire est l'action par excellence.

25. Ibid., p. 432: Triomphera donc cette révolution commencée par Gutemberg, dont on s'apercevra que quatre siècles n'ont fait que balbutier indéfiniment la première phrase.

26. See *Répertoire III*, p. 403; *Répertoire IV*, pp. 441–43.

27. "Imaginez," in *Le Poème Electronique de Le Corbusier* (Paris: Editions du Minuit, 1958), p. 107: ces villes futures où aux principaux carrefours d'uniques édifices instruments . . . joueraient ou vous permettraient de jouer d'irremplaçables contrepoints vous envahissant par tous les sens, où l'histoire du monde, la volonté des hommes se réfléchirait, se découvrirait différemment en chaque lieu, où la variété de notre paysage mental se serait augmentée d'une dimension l'illuminant.

28. *Répertoire II*, p. 19: Le mouvement de la pensée poétique, d'abord retour vers un certain passé perdu, va être indéfiniment renvoyé plus loin, à tel point qu'il ne pourra trouver de repos qu'en dehors du monde et du temps, *anywhere out of the world*, dans une utopie, ou une "uchronie" . . . dans cet en dehors de l'histoire qui va se présenter justement comme "ce que nous désirons". Cette réminiscence et cette nostalgie débouchent soudain sur notre avenir. Ainsi la poésie, critique de la vie présente, nous propose-t-elle son changement.

Conclusion

1. See *Correspondances 1853–1856*, ed. Maurice Nadeau (Lausanne: Editions Rencontre, 1964), p. 409.

2. Robert Scholes, *Structural Fabulation* (South Bend, Ind.: Univ. of Notre Dame Press, 1975), p. 33.

3. "The Ideology of Modernism," in *Backgrounds to Modern Literature*, ed. John Oliver Perry (San Francisco: Chandler Pubs. Co., 1968), p. 263.

4. "The Myth and the Powerhouse," in *Myth and Literature*, ed. John B. Vickery (Lincoln: Univ. of Nebraska Press, 1966), p. 117.

5. "The Modern as a Vision of a Whole Situation," in Perry ed., *Backgrounds to Modern Literature*, p. 232.

6. *Correspondances 1853–1856*, p. 395: encyclopédies de leur époque.

7. Quoted by Harvey Gross, *The Contrived Corridor: History and Fatality in Modern Literature* (Ann Arbor: Univ. of Michigan Press, 1971), p. 100.

8. *L'Arc*, no. 39 (1969), p. 2: L'oeuvre d'un individu est une sorte de noeud qui se produit à l'intérieur d'un tissu culturel au sein duquel l'individu se trouve non pas plongé mais *apparu*. L'individu est, dès l'origine, un moment de ce tissu culturel.

9. "Le Nouveau roman," text of lecture mimeographed by Centre Européen Universitaire, Nancy, Session 1962-63, p. 10: les grands romans du XXe siècle ont existé.

10. *Space, Time and Structure in the Modern Novel* (New York: New York Univ. Press, 1971), pp. xix-xx.

11. See "Une Chanson pour Don Juan," *Degrés, Revue de synthèse à orientation sémiologique*, I. 1 (Jan. 1973), pp. 1-10.

12. See Maria Craipeau "Rencontre avec Michel Butor," *France-Observateur*, no. 394 (25 Nov. 1957), p. 17; "Le Rôle de l'écrivain: Michel Butor et Alain Robbe-Grillet ne sont pas d'accord," *L'Express*, VII, 423 (23 July 1959), 26; Craipeau, "Entretien avec Michel Butor," *France-Observateur*, no. 506 (14 Jan. 1960), 19; J. Delume, "Michel Butor vous parle," *Université de Grenoble. Faculté des lettres et sciences humaines. Service de documentation. Bulletin d'information* (Oct.-Dec. 1968), p. 6.

13. See *Nouveau Roman: hier, aujourd'hui*, (Paris: Union Générale d'Editions, 1972), 2: 279-82.

14. See Bruce Morrissette, "Post-Modern Generative Fiction: Novel and Film," *Critical Inquiry* 2, no. 2 (Winter 1975): 260-62.

15. *Literary Disruptions: The Making of Post-Contemporary American Fiction* (Urbana: Univ. of Illinois Press, 1975), p. 2.

16. *The Nouveau Roman* (Philadelphia: Temple Univ. Press, 1972), p. 219.

17. *Surfiction* (Chicago: Swallow Press, 1975), pp. 8-9.

18. "Une 'lecture' américaine de *Mobile*," *Le Monde*, no. 6902 (22 March 1967), p. 4.

19. For another account of Butor's relationship to modernism and postmodernism see Laura R. Kubinyi, "Defense of a Dialogue: Michel Butor's *Passing Time*," *Boundary 2*, 4, no. 3 (Spring 1976), 885-903.

Bibliography

Works by Michel Butor

I. BOOKS

Passage de Milan. Paris: Editions de Minuit, 1954.

L'Emploi du temps. Paris: Editions de Minuit, 1956. Translated by Jean Stewart as *Passing Time.* New York: Simon & Schuster, 1960.

La Modification. Paris: Editions de Minuit, 1957. Translated by Jean Stewart as *A Change of Heart.* New York: Simon & Schuster, 1959.

Le Génie du lieu. Paris: Grasset, 1958.

Degrés. Paris: Gallimard, 1960. Translated by Richard Howard as *Degrees.* New York: Simon & Schuster, 1962.

Répertoire, Etudes et conférences 1948–1959. Paris: Editions de Minuit, 1960.

Histoire extraordinaire, essai sur un rêve de Baudelaire. Paris: Gallimard, 1961. Translated by Richard Howard as *Histoire Extraordinaire, Essays on a Dream of Baudelaire's.* London: Jonathan Cape, 1969.

Mobile, étude pour une représentation des Etats-Unis. Paris: Gallimard, 1962. Translated by Richard Howard as *Mobile.* New York: Simon & Schuster, 1963.

Réseau aérien, texte radiophonique. Paris: Gallimard, 1962.

Description de San Marco. Paris: Gallimard, 1963.

Hérold. Paris: George Fall, 1964.

Illustrations. Paris: Gallimard, 1964.

Répertoire II, Etudes et conférences 1959–1963. Paris: Editions de Minuit, 1964. Translated as *Inventory.* Edited and with a foreward by Richard Howard. New York: Simon & Schuster, 1968. [Translations by various hands of essays primarily from *Répertoire I* and *II.*]

6.810.000 Litres d'eau par seconde, étude stéréophonique. Paris: Gallimard, 1965. Translated by Elinor S. Miller as *Niagara: A Stereophonic Novel.* Chicago: Henry Regnery Company, 1969.

Portrait de l'artiste en jeune singe, cappricio. Paris: Gallimard, 1967.

Essais sur les Essais. Paris: Gallimard, 1968.

Répertoire III. Paris: Editions de Minuit, 1968.

L'Arc, no. 39 (1969). [Special Butor issue, edited by Butor.]

Illustrations II. Paris: Gallimard, 1969.

Les Mots dans la peinture. Geneva: Skira, 1969.

La Rose des Vents, 32 rhumbs pour Charles Fourier. Paris: Gallimard, 1970.

Dialogue avec 33 variations de Ludwig van Beethoven sur une valse de Diabelli. Paris: Gallimard, 1971.

Où, le Génie du lieu, 2. Paris: Gallimard, 1971.

Rabelais, ou c'était pour rire. In collaboration with Denis Hollier. Paris: Librairie Larousse, 1972.

Les Petits Miroirs. Paris: Editions la Farandole, 1972.

Travaux d'approche. Paris: Gallimard, 1972.

Illustrations III. Paris: Gallimard, 1973.

Intervalle. Paris: Gallimard, 1973.

Michel Butor. Edited by François Aubral. Paris: Editions Seghers, 1973. [Anthology of Butor's poetry.]

Répertoire IV. Paris: Editions de Minuit, 1974.

Matière de rêves. Paris: Gallimard, 1975.

Illustrations IV. Paris: Gallimard, 1976.

Second sous-sol, Matière de rêves 2. Paris: Gallimard, 1976.

Tout l'oeuvre peint de Mondrian. In collaboration with Maria Grazia Ottolenghi. Paris: Flammarion, 1976.

Obliques, February, 1976. [Special Butor and Masurovsky issue, written and illustrated by Butor and Gregory Masurovsky.]

The remaining portion of the bibliography lists only those materials not included in one of the above volumes.

II. ARTICLES

"*Le Préau* par Georges Borgeaud." *Monde nouveau-paru* 8, no. 59 (1952): 58–60.

"*Jean Santeuil* par Marcel Proust, *L'Elu* par Thomas Mann, *Les Poésies* par Georges Schéhadé, *La Philosophie de Virginia Woolf* par Maxime Chastaing." *Monde nouveau-paru* 8, no. 62 (1952): 73–75, 80–81, 92–93, 99.

"*Sainte Barbegrise* par Noel Devaulx." *Monde nouveau-paru* 8, no. 63 (1952): 81.

"*Celui qui ne m'accompagnait pas* par Maurice Blanchot." *La Nouvelle Revue française* 2, no. 8 (Aug. 1953): 331–32.

"Jean Ferry: *Une Etude sur Raymond Roussel*, précédée de *Fronton Virage* par André Breton." *La Nouvelle Revue française* 3, no. 16 (April 1954): 711–13.

"Les Européens et Les Bostoniennes." *Monde nouveau-paru* 11, no. 94 (Nov. 1955): 136–39.

"Une Oeuvre solitaire." *Monde nouveau-paru* 12, no. 98 (March 1956): 91–96.

"Le Roman est un laboratoire du récit." *Les Lettres française*, no. 661 (7 March, 1957), pp. 1, 3.

"Maryvonne et le wagon maudit." *France-Observateur*, no. 389 (24 Oct. 1957), pp. 15–16.

"Mon Journal à l'heure des prix." *Arts*, no. 647 (4 Dec. 1957), p. 4.

"Bienvenue à Duke Ellington, maître du raffinement et de l'ironie." *Arts*, no. 694 (29 Oct. 1958), pp. 1, 9.

"Grand Prix 58 de la photo aux USA: Henri Cartier-Bresson sous l'objectif de Michel Butor." *Arts*, no. 699 (3 Dec. 1958), p. 5.

"Imaginez." In *Le Poème electronique de Le Corbusier*, pp. 103–7. Paris: Edition de Minuit, 1958.

"L'Ecriture, pour moi, est une colonne vertébrale." *Les Nouvelles littéraires*, no. 1640 (5 Feb. 1959), pp. 1, 7.

"Palerme." *L'Arc*, no. 6 (April 1959), pp. 77–80.

"Les Libertés du romanesque." *Arts*, no. 717 (8 April 1959), p. 3.

"À Paris." *L'Oeil français*, no. 54 (June 1959), pp. 34–42.

"*Le Planétarium*, le jeu compliqué des paroles et des silences." *Arts*, no. 725 (3 June 1959), p. 2.

"Le Roman, l'épreuve du temps." *Arts*, no. 732 (22 July 1959), p. 3.

"*Max Ernst* de Patrick Waldeberg." *Critique*, no. 151 (Dec. 1959), pp. 1049–59.

"Les Machines sont des liens entre nous." In *Les Peintres témoins de leur temps: L'Age méchanique*, pp. 66–71. Paris: Musée Galliéra, 1959.

"Pour Gregory Masurowsky." *Pour l'Art*, no. 75 (Nov.–Dec. 1960), pp. 12–15.

"Première vue de Philadelphie." *Les Lettres nouvelles* 8, no. 9 (Dec. 1960): 153–55.

"Des Jeunes Gens de mauvais goût." *Les Lettres françaises*, no. 856 (29 Dec. 1960), p. 1.

"L'Art contemporain jugé par ses sources." *Les Lettres nouvelles* 9, no. 11 (Feb. 1961): 124–39.

"Joyce et le roman moderne." *Les Lettres françaises*, no. 863 (16 Feb. 1961), pp. 1, 3.

"Athalie (927–877 av. J. C.)." *Mercure de France*, no. 1172 (April 1961), pp. 669–71.

"Rencontre avec Antonioni." *Les Lettres françaises*, no. 880 (15 June 1961), pp. 1, 7.

"Kujawski à Darmstadt." *Les Lettres nouvelles* 9, no. 16 (July 1961): 140–43.

"Conversation dans l'atelier: Bernard Saby." *L'Oeil*, nos. 79–80 (July–Aug. 1961), pp. 36–43.

"La Peinture se repeuple." *Figures*, no. 1 (Sept. 1961), pp. 4–21.

"Qu'est-ce que la pornographie." *Les Lettres françaises*, no. 894 (28 Sept. 1961), pp. 1, 6.

"Michel Butor relit Cervantès." *Les Nouvelles littéraires*, no. 1779 (5 Oct. 1961), pp. 1, 6.

"Votre Faust, fantaisie variable, genre opéra." With Henri Pousseur. *La Nouvelle Revue française* 10, nos. 109, 110, 111, 112 (Jan.–April 1962): 65–86, 261–89, 461–82, 641–57. Additional variations in *L'VII*, no. 10 (June 1962), pp. 9–43; *Profils*, no. 2 (Nov. 1962), pp. 23–25; *Méditations*, no. 6 (Summer 1963), pp. 5–19; *Cahiers de la Compagnie Renaud-Barrault*, no. 42 (Feb. 1963), p. 114–17, no. 41 (Dec. 1963), pp. 203–15, *Cahiers du centre d'études et de recherches marxistes*, no. 62 (1968); *Obliques* 1, no. 4 (1973): 131–34; *Marche Romane* 10, no. 3 (1970): 21–37.

"*L'Attente l'oubli* de Maurice Blanchot." *Le Monde*, no. 5409 (9 June 1962), p. 15.

"Bernard Dufour, Au gouffré du modèle." *Vingtième Siècle* 24, no. 19 (June 1962): 89–92.

"William Faulkner: Son pays a mis longtemps à le comprendre." *Le Figaro littéraire*, no. 847 (14 July 1962), p. 8.

"Le Roman européen depuis 1945, Les Grands Courants de l'evolution de l'Europe depuis 1945." Session 1962–63. Distributed by Centre Européen Universitaire, Nancy. Mimeographed, 23 pp.

"Oedipus Americanus." Preface to William Styron, *La Proie des flammes*, pp. vii–xx. Translated by M. E. Coindreau. Paris: Gallimard, 1962.

"Michel Butor a-t-il tiré Claude Monet vers l'informel?" *Les Lettres françaises*, no. 965 (14 Feb. 1963), p. 1.

"La peinture surréaliste." *Cahier bicolore*, no. 4 (March 1963), pp. 23–28.

"Conversation dans l'atelier: Bernard Dufour." *L'Oeil*, no. 100 (April 1963), pp. xvi, 35–40.

"Gadda." *L'Express*, no. 621 (9 May 1963), p. 33.

"Conversations dans l'atelier avec Paul Jenkins." *Cimaise*, no. 65 (July–Oct. 1963), pp. 14–16.

"The Debt." *The Times Literary Supplement*, 4 June 1964, p. 469.

"Pierre Klossowski en discussion: Une Vocation suspendue." *Le Monde*, no. 6513 (19 June 1965), p. 14.

"Les Tendances du roman français après la dernière guerre." *Neusprachliche Mitteilungen aus Wissenschaft und Praxis*, no. 4 (15 Aug. 1966), pp. 193–207.

"L'Oeil de Michel Butor sur Canaletto." *Realités*, no. 258 (July 1967), pp. 36–43.

"Où j'apprends." *Le Français dans le monde* 10, no. 77 (Dec. 1970): 8–9.

"Masurovsky: un entretien avec Michel Butor." *Opus International*, no. 26 (June 1971), pp. 65–66.

"Commenté par Michel Butor: Entre les *Mille et une nuits* et *Barbe-bleue*." *Le Monde*, no. 8237 (9 July 1971), p. 15.

"Influences de formes musicales sur quelques oeuvres, Les Mots dans la musique." *Musique en jeu*, no. 4 (Oct. 1971), pp. 63–72.

"Centre d'écoute, oeuvre où la musique joue un role déterminant." Paris: ORTF atelier pour la création radiophonique, 9 July 1972. Mimeographed, 18 pp.

"Comment se sont écrits certains de mes livres." In *Nouveau roman: hier aujourd 'hui*, ed. Jean Ricardou and Françoise van Rossum-Guyon, 2: 243–54. Paris: Union Générale d'Editions, 1972.

"Composition littéraire et composition musicale." *Communications et langages*, no. 13 (1972), pp. 30–34.

"Les Paravent." *Obliques*, no. 2 (1972), pp. 54–59.

"Propos sur l'écriture et la typographie." *Communications et langages*, no. 13 (1972), pp. 5–29.

"Fantaisie chromatique à propos de Stendhal." *Les Cahiers du chemin*, no. 21 (15 April 1974), pp. 86–114.

"Le Rêve de l'huître." *Cahiers du chemin*, no. 22 (15 Oct. 1974), pp. 55–74.

"Marges pour l'Apocalypse." In *Le Gloire de Dürer*, pp. 205–16. Paris: Klinck-sieck, 1974.

"Francis Ponge: Presentation to the Jury." *Books Abroad* 48 (Autumn 1974): 658.

"Ecorché vif." In *Butor*, pp. 435-50. Proceedings of the Colloque de Cerisy edited by Françoise van Rossum-Guyon. Paris: Union Générale d'Editions, 1974.

"Reproduction interdite." *Critique*, no. 334 (March 1975), pp. 269–83.

"Comment écrire *Boomerang*," *Les Nouvelles littéraires*, no. 2575 (10 March 1977), p. 21.

"Archipel Shopping 1," *L'Arc*, no. 68 (1977), pp. 89–96.

III. INTERVIEWS (including contributions to symposia and responses to questionaires)

"Pourquoi et comment lisez-vous." *Cercle ouvert*, no. 1 (9 Oct. 1956), p. 5.

"Cinq minutes avec Michel Butor." Interview by Dominique Arban. *Le Figaro littéraire*, no. 552 (17 Nov. 1956), p. 12.

"Instané." Interview by André Bourin. *Les Nouvelles littéraires*, no. 1533 (17 Jan. 1957), p. 17.

"Rencontre avec Michel Butor." Interview by Maria Craipeau. *France-Observateur* 8, no. 394 (28 Nov. 1957): 17.

"Les Enfants du demi-siècle: Michel Butor." Interview by André Bourin. *Les Nouvelles littéraires*, no. 1579 (5 Dec. 1957), p. 9.

"1926–1957 ou Les Modifications de Michel Butor: Un Portrait-Interview." Interview by Paul Guth. *Le Figaro littéraire*, no. 607 (7 Dec. 1957), pp. 1, 4.

"Le Théâtre peut-il aborder l'actualité politique?" *France-Observateur* 9, no. 405 (13 Feb. 1958): 13–14.

"Qu'est-ce que l'avant-garde en 1958?" *Les Lettres françaises*, no. 713 (13 March 1958), p. 1.

"Cinq écrivains aux prises." Interview by Roger Prioret. *Le Figaro littéraire*, no. 623 (29 March 1958), pp. 1, 7, 9.

"Vers un nouveau romantisme." *Arts*, no. 700 (10 Dec. 1958), p. 3.

"Le Roman est en train de réfléchir sur lui-même." Interview by Anne Villelaur. *Les Lettres françaises*, no. 764 (12 March 1959), pp. 1, 4, 5.

"Messieurs les écrivains êtes-vous vaniteux." *Carrefour*, no. 763 (22 April 1959), p. 12.

"Reflexions de quelques amateurs: Michel Butor, un alibi trop fréquent pour la mauvaise peinture." *Arts*, no. 727 (17 June 1959), p. 8.

"Les Jeunes Romanciers ne sont pas mûrs pour le théâtre." Interview by Pierre Marcabru. *Arts*, no. 727 (1 July 1959), p. 5.

"Le Rôle de l'écrivain: Michel Butor et Alain Robbe-Grillet ne sont pas d'accord." *L'Express* 7, no. 423 (23 July 1959): 25–27.

"Balzac commence sa vraie carrière." *Arts*, no. 745 (21 Oct. 1959), p. 5.

"Cinq jeunes auteurs défendent leur avant-garde." Interview by Pierre Marcabru. *Arts*, no. 747 (4 Nov. 1959), p. 6.

"Qui sera immortel dans vingt ans?" Interview by François Berger. *Arts*, no. 750 (25 Nov. 1959), p. 3.

"Entretien avec Michel Butor." Interview by Maria Craipeau. *France-Observateur*, no. 506 (14 Jan. 1960), p. 19.

"Une Heure de cours de histoire: Une interview de Michel Butor." Interview by

Hubert Juin. *Les Lettres françaises*, no. 807 (14 Jan. 1960), p. 5.

"Entrevistas: Michel Butor y sus claves." Interview by Enrique Canito. *Insula* 15, no. 159 (Feb. 1960): 5.

"Conversa com Michel Butor." Interview by Osman Lins. *Suplemento Literario de "O Estado de Sao Paolo."* 21 May 1960.

"Tolstoi devant les écrivains d'aujourd'hui: Michel Butor." Interview by Hubert Juin. *Les Lettres françaises*, no. 843 (29 Sept. 1960), pp. 1, 4.

"A quoi servez vous? Michel Butor, écrivain." *La Nouvelle Critique*, no. 120 (Nov. 1960), pp. 12–13.

"Michel Butor." In Madeleine Chapsal, *Les Ecrivains en personne*, pp. 55–70. Paris: René Juillard, 1960.

"Pour Cuba." *Les Lettres françaises*, no. 873 (27 April 1961), p. 3.

"L'Opinion des écrivains sur le procès de Jérôme Lindon: Michel Butor." *Les Lettres françaises*, no. 907 (28 Dec. 1961).

"Où allez-vous pour rire?" Interview by Claude Cézan. *Les Nouvelles littéraires*, no. 1795 (25 Jan. 1962), p. 12.

" 'L'Espace du roman,' par M. Michel Butor, échange de vues." *Revue d'Esthetique* 15, no. 1 (Jan. 1962): 91–97.

"Littérature de témoinage ou littérature d'imagination." Interview by André Bourin. *Les Nouvelles littéraires*, no. 1799 (22 Feb. 1962), pp. 6–7.

"Michel Butor commente *Mobile*." Interview by Thérèse De Saint-Phalle. *Le Monde*, no. 5304 (24 Feb. 1962), 11.

"Michel Butor enfante un nouveau monstre: *Mobile*." Interview by Danielle Chadeau. *Démocratie 62*, 8 March 1962, p. 19.

"Entretien: Michel Butor a essayé d'expliquer à Madeleine Chapsal comment utiliser *Mobile*." *L'Express*, no. 561 (15 March 1962), p. 32.

"La Proie des critiques: Un entretien avec William Styron, Michel Butor et M. E. Coindreau." Interview by Annie Brierre. *Les Nouvelles littéraires*, no. 1803 (22 March 1962), p. 8.

"Intervista a Michel Butor." Interview by Paolo Caruso. *Aut Aut*, no. 60 (March 1962), pp. 165–71.

"Résumé des discussions." *Cahiers d'Association internationale des études françaises*, no. 14 (March 1962), pp. 303–5.

"Michel Butor." Interview by Georges Markow-Totevy. *Bucknell Review* 10 (May 1962): 283–91.

"Entretien avec Michel Butor." Interview by F. C. St. Aubyn. *French Review* 36 (Oct. 1962): 12–22.

"Considérez-vous que l'intelligence traverse actuellement une crise?" *Arts*, no. 892 (28 Nov. 1962), p. 18.

"Les Quatres cents ans de Louis le Grand, d'incomparables fantômes." *Le Figaro littéraire*, no. 891 (18 May 1963), p. 15.

"Vous souvenez-vous du héros de Duhamel?" *Arts*, no. 926 (4 Sept. 1963), p. 500.

"Swann l'éternel a cinquante ans: Reconnaissance." *Le Figaro littéraire*, no. 918 (21 Nov. 1963), p. 7.

"Léonce Peillard's s'entretient avec Michel Butor. Michel Butor répond au questionnaire Marcel Proust." *Livres de France* 31, no. 6 (June–July 1963): 6–9.

"Michel Butor: *Répertoire II*." Interview by Jean Gaugeard. *Les Lettres françaises*, no. 1022 (26 March 1964), p. 4.

"Pierre Daix avec Michel Butor: Pour moi, l'important c'est de devenir contemporain." *Les Lettres françaises*, no. 1037 (9 July 1964), pp. 1, 6–7.

"Les Réactions" [of writers on L. F. Céline]. *Le Nouvel Observateur*, no. 15 (25 Feb. 1965), pp. 27–28.

"A propos de *Mobile*: Deuxième entretien avec Michel Butor." Interview by F. C. St. Aubyn. *French Review* 38, no. 4 (Feb. 1965): 427–40.

"Michel Butor." Interview by Denise Bourdet. *La Revue de Paris* 72, no. 10 (Nov. 1965): 127–33.

"Les Etats-Unis et mon livre *Mobile*." Recorded interview with Hughes Desalle. Collection Français de Notre Temps, no. 57, apparently recorded in 1965.

"L'Image du monde au 19e siècle." *Arts-Loisirs*, no. 27 (30 March 1966), pp. 9–10.

"Le Plus Grand Auteur du XXe siècle avec Beckett?" Interview by Pierre Hahn. *Arts-Loisirs*, no. 28 (6 April 1966), p. 17.

"Le Nouveau Roman." Butor's response to questions at the Seminaire sur le nouveau roman, 27 April 1966. Distributed by the Centre Européen Universitaire, Nancy. Mimeographed, 22 pp.

"Trois devant Zola." *Arts-Loisirs*, no. 57 (26 Oct. 1966), pp. 29–30.

"Incontro con Michel Butor, autore della 'Modificazione': Un Ingegnere alla ricerca della realtà perduta." Interview by Claudio Barbati. *La Fiera letteraria* 40, no. 43 (3 Nov. 1966): 7.

"Le Livre futur: entretien avec Michel Butor." Interview by Henri Ronse. *Synthèses* 22, no. 248 (Jan. 1967): 101–7.

"Entretien avec Michel Butor." Interview by Martine Cadieu. *Les Lettres françaises*, no. 1167 (2 Feb. 1967), pp. 16–17.

"La Revanche de Zola." Interview by Roger Borderie. *Le Nouvel Observateur*, no. 122 (15 March 1967), pp. 32–33.

"Butor s'explique." Interview by Jacqueline Piatier. *Le Monde*, no. 6902 (22 March 1967), p. 5.

"Les Meilleurs Livres de l'année 1966." *Le Français dans le monde*, no. 47 (March 1967), p. 45.

"Michel Butor: 'Je ne suis pas un iconoclaste.' " Interview by Henri Ronse. *Les Lettres françaises*, no. 1178 (13 April 1967), pp. 5–7.

"Opinions recueillies par Pierre Hahn: Onze écrivains et éditeurs nous disent ce qu'ils pensent de la littérature érotique." *Magazine littéraire*, no. 13 (Dec. 1967), pp. 20–23.

Entretiens avec Michel Butor. Edited by Georges Charbonnier. Paris: Gallimard, 1967.

"Michel Butor à Grenoble." Interview by Madeleine Chapsal. *La Quinzaine littéraire*, no. 44 (Feb. 1968), pp. 14–15.

"Dramaturgie pour un théâtre mobile: Un entretien avec Michel Butor."

146   NARRATIVES OF MICHEL BUTOR

Interview by Roger Borderie and Henri Ronse. *Les Lettres françaises*, no. 1225 (13 March 1968), pp. 14–15.

"Vers un enseignement universel: Un entretien avec Michel Butor." Interview by Pierre Jeancard. *Liberté* 10, no. 2 (March–April 1968): 33–37.

"Michel Butor vous parle." Interview by J. Delume. *Université de Grenoble. Faculté des lettres et sciences humaines. Service de documentation. Bulletin d'information* (Oct.–Dec. 1968), pp. 3–9.

"Entretien avec Henri Pousseur et Michel Butor." *Cahiers du Centre d'études et de recherche marxistes*, no. 62 (1968), pp. 32–35.

"Entretien avec Michel Butor." In Georges Raillard, *Butor*, pp. 263–69. Paris: Gallimard, 1968.

"Le Nouvel Opéra: Entretien avec Michel Butor et Henri Pousseur." Interview by Martine Cadieu. *Les Nouvelles littéraires*, no. 2159 (6 Feb. 1969), p. 11.

"Michel Butor, Marc Albert-Levin: Dialogue à propos de 'Un printemps à New York.' " *Les Lettres françaises*, no. 1285 (28 May 1969), pp. 3–5.

"Un Art nouveau? Michel Butor nous éclaire sur les recherches d'aujourd'hui." Interview by Gilles Quéant. *Plaisir de France* 35, no. 368 (June 1969), pp. 1–8.

"A Talk by Michel Butor." *Prism International* 9, no. 2 (Autumn 1969): 62–75.

"Entretien avec Michel Butor." Interview by Roger Borderie. *Les Lettres françaises*, no. 1315 (31 Dec. 1969), pp. 7–8.

"La remise en question du personnage: Les Faux-Monnayeurs et le nouveau roman." Interview by Margaret Pilcer. [Followed by interviews with Alain Robbe-Grillet, Natalie Sarraute, and Butor]. Master's thesis, University of Paris, 1969.

"Dialogues sur les villes: Interviews de Michel Butor et J. M. G. Le Clezio." Interview by Denis Goldschmidt. *L'Architecture d'aujourd'hui*, no. 153 (Dec. 1970), pp. 4–7.

"Parole vere e parole ingannatrici." Interview by Pier Francesco Listri. *Appropodo letterario* 16, no. 53 (1970): 109–12.

"Michel Butor a réponse à tous." Interview by Bernard Pivot. *Le Figaro littéraire*, no. 1307 (4 June 1971), p. 11.

"Comment travaillent les écrivains: Michel Butor." Interview by Jean-Louis de Rambures. *Le Monde*, no. 8213 (11 June 1971), p. 24.

"Entretien avec Michel Butor: La Littérature, fille du roman. Un rempart contre le monde." Interview by Guy Le Clec'h. *Les Nouvelles littéraires*, no. 2283 (25 June 1971), p. 9.

"Michel Butor en 40 questions." *La Galérie*, no. 106 (July 1971), pp. 64–65.

"Interview with Michel Butor." Interview by Stephen Bann. *20th Century Studies*, no. 6 (Dec. 1971), pp. 41–52.

"8 Questions à Michel Butor." Interview by Danielle Bajomée. *Marche Romane* 21, nos. 1–2 (1971): 37–39.

"Questionnaire de M. Jolas adressé à M. Butor." *Rencontres artistiques et littéraires*, no. 5 (June 1972), p. 12.

"Michel Butor devant ses juges." Interview by Jacqueline Piatier. *Le Monde*, no. 8737 (15 Feb. 1973), pp. 17–18.

"Un Passe-muraille nommé Butor." Interview by Jacques Michel. *Le Monde*, no. 8889 (20 July 1973), p. 11.

"Du Mouvement en littérature, entretien avec Michel Butor." Interview by Anne Fabre-Luce. *Cahiers du XXᵉ siècle*, no. 1 (1973), pp. 7–23.

"Une Question à Michel Butor." *Obliques* 1, no. 4 (1973): 3–6.

"An Interview with Michel Butor." Interview by Jack Kolbert. *American Society of the Legion of Honor Magazine* 45, no. 2 (1974): 90–93.

"On *Passing Time*." *Mosaic* 8, no. 1 (Fall 1974): 33–37, 48–50.

"Dialogue avec Michel Butor." In André Helbo, *Michel Butor: vers une littérature du signe*, pp. 9–15. Brussels: Editions Complexe, 1975.

"Entretien avec Michel Butor." Interview by Robert Mélançon. *Etudes françaises* 11, no. 1 (Feb. 1975): 67–91.

"Pour Michel Butor les frontières entre science-fiction et littérature tendent à s'effacer." Interview by Xavier Delcourt. *La Quinzaine littéraire*, no. 225 (16 Jan. 1976), pp. 5–7.

IV. POETRY

"Hommage partiel à Max Ernst." *Vrille, La peinture et la littérature surréaliste.* Mantes: Editions du Petit Mantais, 1945.

"Poèmes anciens." *Les Lettres nouvelles* 7, no. 68 (Feb. 1959): 190–202.

"Souvenirs d'enfance." *L'VII*, no. 5 (21 April 1961), pp. 9–30.

"Diorama pour le muséum 1948." *Shi'r* (Beirut), no. 18 (Spring 1961).

"La Banlieue de l'aube à l'aurore." *L'VII*, no. 10 (Spring 1962), pp. 44–57.

"Trois Hommages." *Cahiers du Sud* 61, nos. 387–88 (April–June 1966): 227–32.

"Conditionnement. Pour Edmund Alleyn." *Opus International*, no. 3 (Oct. 1967), pp. 39–43.

"Flic, Flac." *Le Monde*, no. 7272 (1 June 1968), p. 11.

"Trouble, tremble, transparent, trille." *L'Arbre, Revue mondiale de poésie*, nos. 8–9 (July–Oct. 1968), pp. 7–12.

Tourmente. Montpelier: Fata Morgana, 1968.

"Eclats." *MELE, International Poetry Letter*, March 1969.

"Les Paranthèses de l'été." *Encres vives*, no. 67 (Autumn–Winter, 1969).

"Fable." In *Calder.* Saint Paul: Fondation Maeght, 1969, pp. 13–15.

"Jalons, pour H. M. Erhardt. Ressac, pour Vieira da Silva. Champs de vitres, pour Cesare Peverelli. Voix de l'écrit: Cantate optique pour saluer les logogrammes de Christian Dotremont." *La Nouvelle Revue française* 28, no. 212 (1 Aug. 1970): 17–25.

"La Politique des charmeuses." *Topique*, nos. 4–5 (1970), pp. 99–101.

"Zoo." *Avant-Quart*, no. 9 (1970).

"Perle, pour France Gaspar." *Métamorphoses*, nos. 15–17 (May 1971).

"Lettre à Jean-Luc Parant." *Obliques*, no. 1 (1972), p. 105.

"Don Juan dans l'Essonne." *Métamorphoses*, nos. 19–20 (Winter 1972–73), pp. 136–41.

"Une Chanson pour Don Juan." *Degrés, Revue de synthèse à orientation sémiologique* 1, no. 1 (Jan. 1973): 1–10.

"Don Juan dans les Yvelines." *Obliques* 1, no. 4 (1973): 2–14, 27–62, 135–46.

Books on Butor's Works

Albérès, R.-M. *Butor*. Paris: Editions Universitaires, 1964.

Colloque de Cerisy edited by Françoise van Rossum-Guyon. *Butor*. Paris: Union Générale d'Editions, 1974.

Dällenbach, Lucien. *Le Livre et ses miroirs dans l'oeuvre romanesque de Michel Butor*. Paris: Les Archives des Lettres Modernes, 1972.

Helbo, André. *Michel Butor: vers une littérature du signe*. Brussels: Editions Complexe, 1975.

Raillard, Georges. *Butor*. Paris: Gallimard, 1968.

Roudaut, Jean. *Michel Butor ou le livre futur*. Paris: Gallimard, 1964.

Roudiez, Leon S. *Michel Butor*. New York: Columbia Univ. Press, 1965.

Spencer, Michael C. *Michel Butor*. New York: Twayne Publishers, 1974.

Van Rossum-Guyon, Françoise. *Critique du roman. Essai sur "La Modification" de Michel Butor*. Paris: Gallimard, 1970.

Waelti-Walters, Jennifer, *Alchimie et littérature. A propos de Portrait de l'artiste en jeune singe*. Paris: Denoël, 1975.

Wolfzettel, Friedrich. *Michel Butor und der Kollektivroman*. Heidelberg: Carl Winter Universitätsverlag, 1969.

Index

149